Advance Praise for *The* W9-BMB-884

"*The Happiness Factor* teaches us that being happy or not is a *choice* and not a consequence or reaction to circumstance. We can always have the power to rise above our emotions and fly. Edifying and inspiring!"

> —Stephen R. Covey, author of *The 7 Habits of Highly Effective People* and *The 8th Habit: From Effectiveness to Greatness*

"No matter what challenges you are facing—in your relationships, career, business or life—*The Happiness Factor* is bound to help you live a more rewarding, joyful, and happy life. Buy it, read it, live it!"

> —Margie Warrell, coach, speaker, and author of *Find Your Courage! Unleash Your Full Potential and Live the Life You Really Want*

"You don't need to wait for anything or anyone else to be happy. You can be happy right now! Read and use this book to learn how."

> —Michele Wing, M.Ed., licensed professional counselor

"Life is full of complex decisions, tough negotiations, and important conflicts. In *The Happiness Factor*, Kirk Wilkinson provides a powerful way of successfully managing these challenges through a fresh and insightful approach to developing and sustaining personal happiness."

> —Jeff Weiss, founding partner of Vantage Partners, LLC, and past member of the Harvard Negotiation Project

"Happy people are healthier, have more energy and radiate beauty from the inside out. Kirk Wilkinson empowers each of us to be happy and fulfilled in any situation and any circumstance. You will love this book!"
—Cynthia Rowland, creator of Facial Magic

"What an inspirational, encouraging, *and practical* book! Turning the P-E-A-S-E-F-U-L framework toward the workplace, imagine how much more productive, creative, and collaborative we could be in business if we operated from a level of trust and self-propelled happiness. Let's all read this book and find out!"

—Carrie Welles, vice president of Think! Inc. and board member of Strategic Account Management Association (SAMA)

The
HAPPINESS
Factor

How to Be Happy
No Matter What!

Kirk Wilkinson

The Happiness Factor: How to Be Happy No Matter What!
Published by Ovation Books
P.O. Box 80107
Austin, TX 78758

For more information about our books, please write to us, call 512.478.2028, or visit our website at www.ovationbooks.net

Distributed to the trade by National Book Network, Inc.

Publisher's Cataloging-in-Publication
(Provided by Quality Books, Inc.)

    Wilkinson, Kirk, 1957-
      The happiness factor : how to be happy no matter
  what! / Kirk Wilkinson.
      p. cm.
      Includes bibliographical references.
      LCCN 2008923962
      ISBN-13: 978-0-9814534-0-8
      ISBN-10: 0-9814534-0-6

      1. Happiness.   I. Title.

  BF575.H27W55 2008   158.1
                    QBI08-600096

Cover design by Kristy Buchanan

To God and my family. Be happy—be the miracle.

To ERIC.
Be happy every day!

Kirk Wilkinson

Table of Contents

A personal note

Most people are very interested in the subject of happiness. While some are eager to learn and apply the Happiness Factor, others are interested because someone they know can benefit from it. There are those I have met whose mental image of what it means to be happy is so foreign they have a hard time seeing themselves that way. I have even met people who I would say don't need this book. I firmly believe that if you are ready, the principles in this book can help you be happy or happier than you are today. I know this from what I have experienced in my own life and in the lives of those whom I have had the privilege of helping.

As I share the principles of the Happiness Factor, I am invariably asked if I am still happy. The answer is yes. Being happy is a process, not an event. It is a journey, not a destination. It is not where you arrive, it is how you get there. As a happy person, I still have ups and downs, good days and bad. I still need to apply the principles shared in this book. I have the same challenges that most of you do and the same problems that most people have. The difference is that the low moods and problems are less intense and easier to manage. They are literally dissolved as I apply the Happiness Factor.

My overall satisfaction with life has increased a hundred-fold, and yet my circumstances have changed very little. My relationship with my wife is better than it has ever been, my children find me more approachable and financial and career setbacks are no longer debilitating. My feelings are not hurt as often. I have greater confidence at work and in social situations.

For me, the Happiness Factor has the greatest impact when practiced on a daily basis and sometimes more than once a day. Though I am the one who wrote this book, I often review and rededicate myself to the principles of the Happiness Factor, and I use the P·E·A·S·E·F·U·L framework to easily remember and apply them. In those instances when I feel negativity and unhappiness creep back into my life, when I start to have problems, stress and worry, it is usually because I have tried to resolve it on my own rather than applying the Happiness Factor. I am happy, and through the principles in this book, I believe I have the tools to be happy forever. I am confident that you too will be happy applying the Happiness Factor.

Be happy!

Be the miracle!

Acknowledgments

The Happiness Factor came about by miraculous means. From the kind words of a friend that had a tremendous impact upon me to the many doors that have opened to help this book come to fruition there are too many miracles to list individually. I am grateful for the people and these miracles that have enabled me to complete this work and share it with you.

I am deeply grateful for the friends, family, clients, and colleagues that have both encouraged me and allowed me to share the concepts of this book. Their kind and direct feedback has helped it become a much better work than it would have been otherwise. I am also grateful to those who have become passionate sponsors for this work.

I am particularly grateful for my dear wife Karen for her unwavering patience, love, and support through my personal trials and learning. I am so glad we are together, and I look forward to many great years ahead.

There are a few other people that deserve particular acknowledgement and my expression of gratitude:

To my daughter Meghan who was the first to read the initial draft of the book and provided great insight, very direct feedback, and encouragement to continue.

To Jeff Benintendi for his marketing and graphic arts expertise and broad network of friends and acquaintances.

To Mark P. Durham, CEO of Imaginisce Inc., for his encouragement and support.

To Stephen R. Covey for his generous advice and council.

Additionally, I would like to thank my editor for her dedication and interest in this subject and for helping this book to become more readable and compelling.

Introduction

In the last book of The Chronicles of Narnia written by C. S. Lewis, Aslan the lion, representing God, says, "You do not yet look so happy as I mean you to be."[1] Our own God might say the same thing about us. In my travels, I meet multitudes of people who are not yet as happy as God means them to be. What about you? Are you as happy as God means you to be? Are you happy right now? Regardless of your answer, you can be happier than you are right now. If you are experiencing stress, worry, concern or find yourself facing adversity and negativity, all of that can be dissolved, and you can be happy. You can be happy no matter what.

We each have a different definition and standard for happiness. For some of us, the smallest things like a ray of sunshine or a blossoming rose bring us happiness. For others, happiness is reserved for special and perfect occasions like getting a promotion or a wedding. While everyone wants to be happy, most mistakenly believe that happiness "just happens" and that we are happy as the result of favorable circumstances. However, happiness based on circumstances is fleeting and unreliable. Maybe you were happy before and now you are not. You keep waiting for things to change so you can be happy again. Perhaps you are in the midst of a difficult or devastating situation, and you long for it to be over so you can feel happy again. It could be that you just don't feel satisfied with your life and you feel empty inside. Or, like some, you feel you can never be happy because of something you have done or something that has happened to you.

- Lisa suffers from "supermom syndrome." She feels pressure to be perfect from her husband, children, school, and church and has reached her breaking point. She feels trapped with no way out. She is on the verge of a nervous breakdown and is embarrassed to talk about it. She suffers silently, going on day after day as if nothing is wrong.

- With four small children, Debra has no time for herself. She is constantly cleaning house, picking up toys, and getting criticized by her husband for being messy and a bad cook. She is always tired and questions her decision to be a mother and hates herself for even having those thoughts.

- Larry wonders if this is all there is to life. He had such high hopes for himself, and now he just survives day after day. He and his wife just tolerate each other. The passion is gone, and he doesn't feel anything anymore.

- Last year, Carol's husband left her for another woman. She is raising her five small children alone. "It's all my fault," she says. "If I had been a better wife, this would not have happened." The person she sees in the mirror is hurtful, angry, and unpleasant. She is deeply in debt and cries herself to sleep each night.

- Jessica is a people pleaser. She goes out of her way to please everyone, and she considers herself the family peacemaker. It is her life's work to make sure everyone is okay. If the people around her are unhappy, she is unhappy.

- Paula doesn't understand why her husband and children can't see all that she does for them every day. "I just want to be appreciated," she says. Night after night, she wonders if someone will recognize her for something, if someone will value her and her effort as a wife and mother.

- Andy tells me that he can't do anything. He can't sing, he can't paint—he has no talents. He feels worthless. Everyone else has great things they can do, but not Andy.

- Monica is overweight and has failed diet after diet. She looks in the mirror and hates herself for not having more self-control. It seems that just looking at food causes her to gain weight.

- Patty is distraught over her son who wants nothing to do with her church and values.

- John is the top salesman for his company and receives bonuses and awards each year. Everyone considers him successful because of his nice car, big house, and the money he makes. He tells me he feels unfulfilled, unsatisfied, empty, and emotionally desolate. He feels stuck! He hates his life and hates his career.

- Cassidy was having a great day until her friend was late for an appointment, and it ruined her whole schedule. As each appointment was late, she became angrier.

- Jack is in a "gunk"—a guy funk. He looks at his life and realizes it didn't turn out the way he had expected. He is sad to think that it is too late to change things.

- Maryann watches the news and is depressed about all the bad things happening in the world.

- Andrea is struggling with a family conflict and feels hurt and angry by the people who should be closest to her.

- Randy lost his job of twenty-three years as an accountant. His comment to me was, "I am an accountant. That is not just what I do, it is who I am." He has lost himself because he lost his job.

- Cindy just spent the last hour trying to convince her cell phone carrier that she was overbilled. She is dumbfounded by the incompetence of their customer service department. It has ruined her whole day, and everyone she runs into has to hear the story of how cell phone carriers try to rip you off.

- Terry, now thirty-two, got pregnant at the age of sixteen and gave the baby up for adoption. She regrets getting pregnant and can't forget about the baby.

Our success, peace, satisfaction, and happiness are not about what happens to us but how we deal with what happens to us. You can be happy *now* no matter what, regardless of your circumstances and situation. The adversity, negativity, and pain you experience can be dissolved, empowering you to be happy. We are meant to be as happy as God means us to be. Life is meant to be enjoyable. There is a better way, and the way is the Happiness Factor.

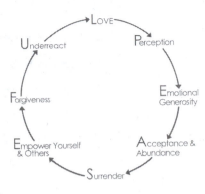

Chapter 1

Choose to be happy

Happiness is not found like some buried treasure. It is about becoming, about being. This "becoming," this "being" is the Happiness Factor. It dissolves negativity, adversity, and the pain of everyday life.

Happiness is found on the inside. It is truly an inside-out phenomenon. This was a hard lesson for me to learn—to look on the inside for my own satisfaction and happiness. Once I learned this simple but powerful principle and made the decision to use it, I became happy. It came down to making a conscious choice to be happy. It meant taking a hard, long look at myself—not at others, not at my circumstances—but directly and deeply at who I had become. Most of us resist learning too much about ourselves because we are afraid that the truth might be too revealing. Instead, we reject feedback and counsel and blame others for our misfortune and dissatisfactions. We often don't recognize when we do this because it has become automatic. Being happy is not found in things; it is found on the inside. Happiness happens from the inside out.

I suppose my story, like the stories in the introduction, is not all that uncommon. You wake up one day and say, "How did I get here? I am not where I want to be!" You wake up to realize that the happiness you wanted is not where you were looking, and the satisfaction and fulfillment you sought are outside of your reach. I used to think that happy people were "over the top" with their happiness and either high on drugs or blind to reality. But it's simply not true. Happiness—lasting happiness—is available to all of us regardless of our background, circumstances, or our mental and physical capacities. I can honestly say I have never been happier than I am right now in this moment. It is not fleeting happiness; it is not momentary or elusive; it is real, powerful, and lasting. The happiness I feel did not come by accident nor did it come after a period of intense therapy or by hiding in seclusion to "find myself." The happiness I feel today, the extreme satisfaction I am experiencing in this moment came by choice—the choice to be happy. You too can make the same choice. If I can be happy, then anyone can. You can be happy! This not about *finding* happiness—happiness is not found like some buried treasure. It is about *becoming*, about *being*. This "becoming," this "being" is the Happiness Factor. It dissolves negativity, adversity, and the pain of everyday life.

Like most of us, my childhood wasn't great. Sure, there were good times, but for the most part, I would say that my childhood held the same challenges as yours. My adult life has had its challenges as well but nothing far from ordinary. I have had to deal with physical and emotional abandonment, losing my job, two bouts of and treatments for cancer, financial problems, and the struggles that come with being a husband and a father to four children. If you were to look at me from the outside, you would say my life is absolutely normal. I have a good wife, productive relationships with my children, active participation in my church congregation, a good job with an adequate income, and after fourteen years in remission from the last bout with cancer, I have manageable health. I am neither overly successful nor am I destitute. I am just an average guy living an average life. But before I discovered the

Happiness Factor, I believed that something was missing. I felt empty, unsatisfied, and unfulfilled.

Even with all the good in my life, I wasn't happy! Of course, I had happy moments like we all do, but they were fleeting and didn't last. Multiple times in my life I found myself in despair, wishing and wanting something more. I began to seriously believe that the life I was living was as good as it would get. Accepting the idea that life wasn't going to get any better was to accept failure; it was depressing. To say I was just having a midlife crisis would be a cliché and would minimize the despair I felt. No matter how I measured success I was failing. My relationship with my wife was suffering, and we found ourselves in and out of counseling. My children were straying from our beliefs and values, and the security I had enjoyed in working for the same company for more than twenty years was now gone. I was feeling tremendous stress at work as we downsized and as I realized that my decisions could impact the fate of my employees. My life was spinning out of control.

No matter how I looked at my life, I was failing—I was failing through mediocrity, through being average, and I felt there was no way out. I was unhappy, and all the hard work and righteous living wasn't bringing me the happiness I desired. I also suffered from "extreme anonymity" or what I call acute loneliness—feeling alone when you are surrounded by people. With a job that required me to travel, not having a lot of close friends, and with my wife suffering depression (it was all she could do to take care of herself), I felt completely alone. My loneliness wasn't because I was physically alone; it was more that I felt that no one knew me and, worse yet, that no one wanted to know me. I felt invisible and anonymous. I felt that if I were to disappear, no one would notice for a long, long time. As a young man I had such high hopes, a tremendous feeling of destiny, and a strong feeling that I would make a difference in the world. But as I got older, reality set in that there was no difference I could make and my destiny was to be average.

When I was eight years old, my mother abandoned me, and I did not see her again until I was twenty-two. Knowing the pain of abandonment, I went out of my way to be there for my own children. Money was tight when I was growing up, so I pushed myself to provide for my wife and children in a way that I never experienced as a child. I tended to be overly supportive as a father, most likely overcompensating for having been abandoned at such a young age.

Yet the more I tried to connect with the people closest to me, the more alone and anonymous I felt. I wanted to be accepted for who I was and to be recognized for the value I added to others' lives instead of always having to change in order to be what people wanted me to be. I wanted everyone and everything else to change so I could find peace and satisfaction. I wanted others to see the value I brought to them both at home and at work. There was such an overwhelming feeling of being alone—of being anonymous to the world—that I battled thoughts of suicide. These thoughts both surprised and frightened me.

Feeling alone while surrounded by people who should love me and be there for me was worse than physical loneliness. I convinced myself that there was no one to turn to. My wife was experiencing depression; I could not turn to her. My father would listen, but it just didn't feel right to confess my failures and disappoint him. I had no relationship with my mother, having only seen her five times since she abandoned me, and I had no friends to whom I could express this without embarrassment. I felt completely and utterly emotionally invisible and alone. I was full of conflict. Was I depressed? Probably, but I don't know. Did I need help? Yes, I did. But I didn't know who to turn to. I started seeing a counselor, and she recommended joint counseling with my wife. It wasn't good timing because of her depression, but it couldn't wait. Rather than finding a solution, the counseling became another way for me to place all the blame on my wife. We tried counseling a year later, and though we were finding common ground, it was a long, hard process focusing mostly on past events and childhood trauma. Inside I was still plotting how to escape the overwhelming sense of failure, hoping that someone would find me valuable so that I could overcome the extreme sense of anonymity. I had lost hope of ever feeling satisfied, feeling joy, and feeling anything other than mediocrity, loneliness, and failure.

Fortunately, a miracle saved me. The adage that says "When the student is ready the teacher will appear" came true for me, and the teacher appeared in the most unlikely of places and from the most unlikely of people—an employee of mine. Joe and I had a rocky start as I challenged him on his performance and considered putting him on probation. To my surprise, he handled the feedback maturely and professionally, and through the intense discussions and meetings, we became close friends. Joe eventually confided in me that he was recovering from drug addiction and was reaching the three year mark of being clean. Joe, a few years older than me, told me that for most of his adult life, he had been a drug addict and had experienced all the ups and downs and devastation associated with addiction. He was still married to his sweetheart of almost thirty years and had a decent relationship with her. He loved his family, and as far as I could tell, they loved him. On top of that, Joe seemed happy and content. Sure there were issues, problems, and adversity in his life, but in spite of those problems and issues, he had a level of contentment that I desired for myself.

The more I learned of Joe's experience and his struggle to get clean, the more I realized that my own problems were nothing compared to his. If he could overcome drug addiction, then I could overcome the curse of mediocrity and anonymity. Though I never really shared the enormity of my problems with Joe, he sensed something was wrong and one day said, "Kirk, your problems are within you, not outside of you. Your problems will be solved from the inside out." He went on to say that happiness is a choice. You can either bemoan your circumstances and the people around you, or you can choose to be happy no matter what.

I had always known this. I had read and internalized many self-help and inspirational books. At a young and impressionable age, I had been exposed to the principles found in Stephen R. Covey's book, *The 7 Habits of Highly Effective People*, and felt they were an integral part of my life. The book had become my handbook for life—my guide and lantern, if you will. My employees considered me to be an excellent manager, and others would say I was confident and an optimist. However, I had forgotten the principles I had once learned, and though I applied them at work and with others, I was not applying them to myself. I had lost my way. I had gotten off the path to happiness and was heading down a dangerous and threatening road. I was heading for disaster. Joe's counsel led me to make the choice to be happy. It is a choice we can all make. In making this choice, I was also led back to many of the principles I had known before and a few I had yet to learn. With gusto I studied and applied them to my life, and they became the greatest factor in my happiness. These principles are the principles of the Happiness Factor.

I have overcome mediocrity and the sense of failure, and I am now happy. This happiness lives, breaths, and lasts. In fact, I am happier than I have ever been. Have any of my circumstances changed? No, not really. My circumstances have only changed as I have changed on the inside. My happiness is not fleeting, it is not momentary; it is long-lasting and true happiness. If this can happen to me, just an average and regular guy, then it can happen to you. This is the Happiness Factor, a set of principles and skills set in an easy-to-remember framework that enables you to be happy regardless of the situation and regardless of the circumstances. The Happiness Factor dissolves all that is negative in your life, all the adversity you experience, and all the pain you are holding inside. You can be happy no matter what.

Seek to be happy

Most of us are quite familiar with the phrase found in the New Testament in the books of Matthew and Luke: "Ask, and it shall be given you; seek, and ye shall find; knock, and it shall be opened unto you: For every one that asketh receiveth; and he that *seeketh findeth*; and to him that knocketh it shall be opened." (Matt. 7:7–8; Luke 11:9; italics added) What powerful words. In Christian religions, these verses are used to teach that God answers prayers. The acts of *a*sking, *s*eeking, and *k*nocking (notice the acronym ASK) combine to offer a simple and powerful formula for receiving God's blessings. Seek and ye shall find! I know this to be true in my own life, and I have experienced this in my relationships with others. We find what we seek. The question then becomes, what are you seeking? When I have asked this question, rarely does anyone readily know what they are looking for. If you really want to know what you are seeking, you need look no further than what you find. For instance, if you find your spouse annoying, then you are actually seeking it. If you find that your coworker is lazy, guess what? You are seeking it; you are actually looking for it and will find all sorts of evidence to support it. In fact, your ego demands that you find it because we all want to be right. The promise is true—you find what you seek. If you find unhappiness, despair, loneliness, or strife, the chances are you are subconsciously seeking those things. Seek happiness, and that is what you will find.

Happiness may seem like a very ambiguous thing to seek. How does one seek happiness? The answer lies within the chapters of this book.

No thing will make you happy

Nothing will make you happy. Happiness comes from the inside. I cannot state it more clearly. In fact, you can also say that *no thing* will make you happy either. Many people live a fantasy, thinking that the next job, the next promotion, a bigger house, car, or some other material thing will bring them happiness. It becomes a never-ending pursuit. Once you achieve what you think will bring you happiness, you may feel fleeting euphoria but not lasting happiness. There have been many studies on this very topic such as the landmark study in 1977 by psychologist Phillip Brickman. He compared lottery winners to quadriplegics to determine which group was happier or had a higher quality of life.[2] At first blush, you would readily think that someone who has millions of dollars and can buy anything they want would find great happiness. The study reported that those people who had lost the use of limbs or even their entire body from the neck down claimed they had a higher quality of life than they did before they were paralyzed. The lottery winners reported a state of excitement and euphoria that soon ended, and their quality of life actually deteriorated. Some of the lottery winners even declared bankruptcy or fell into addictions. *No thing* can bring you happiness. You become happy from the inside out.

If you are like me, your intellect knows that material things don't bring happiness. But my actions didn't follow what I knew intellectually. Sometimes it was more a matter of trying to influence and convince God to grant me happiness by creating favorable circumstances. But circumstances are on the outside, not on the inside. Happiness is not dependant on circumstances, especially ones that you try to create or influence. Regardless of your situation, you can be happy. There are so many people around us who have real and difficult problems who are content and happy, and yet there are so many who are not. The difference is not in the circumstances but what is on the inside.

No thing can bring you happiness. Happiness is living in a way that brings peace and contentment into your life regardless of the circumstances. I have met many successful yet miserable people. People who you would consider successful in every way but who claim they are empty inside. Perhaps you find yourself in that category—successful but unfulfilled, successful but not happy. I was once there! I did not change my job, find a new wife, or move to a different city to be happy. I found it inside of me, and you can find it inside of you!

Happiness can last

We have all experienced happiness at one time or another. You may have a mental list of the times you felt happy. It could have been when you received that promotion you were hoping for, or the award and recognition you felt you deserved. Perhaps it was the moment your sweetheart proposed to you or when your sweetheart accepted your proposal. For most of us, those moments are wonderful and cherished. For me, one of the happiest events in my life was my daughter's wedding. I can't really describe exactly why it was so special to me, but I remember leaving the temple where she was married feeling like the world around me was more beautiful. My heart was full of awe and wonder. Though it was the middle of winter, it felt as if it were spring. I had greater love for everything and everyone around me. It was a tremendous feeling. Just one hour later, as we hurried to the restaurant for the luncheon and then to the church to attend to other wedding chores, I noticed the intense feeling of happiness had left me, and I mourned for its return. I am sure we have all had similar experiences and wondered why the euphoric feeling of happiness didn't last. Is life meant to be a series of sporadic and temporary feelings of happiness? I used to think that, but now I don't! There is a way to have that feeling every day, all day long. It takes work, concentration, and real intent, but it is yours to have; it is yours to become. Like anything, it takes some knowledge and some practice. I offer both to you in this book. In *Secrets of a Satisfying life*, David D. Ireland writes, "Happiness comes when you set a threshold of satisfaction that allows you to feel that an experience was positive. Unhappy people are reluctant to set such a limit because in their minds, happiness only occurs when the experience is perfect."[3] He goes on to say that people who are happy have no difficulty in drawing a positive conclusion from the same experience that others consider negative. We don't need to wait for "special" experiences in order to be happy. It is available to us anytime we want when we learn to find satisfaction in everyday life, in the normal day-to-day things that many people will find boring. Right now, in this very moment, you can be happy.

The choice to be happy

Life is full of choices—sometimes too many choices. We are bombarded with opportunities and decisions that have serious consequences. Choice, the ability to choose, is a gift from God. It sets us apart from all living things on this earth. Animals do not have many choices in their lives. From day to day, one raccoon's life is the same as any other raccoon's. We, however, as humans and God's children, have the gift of choice not available to other living things. Choices such as what career to pursue, what city to live in, and what clothes to wear on a certain day are all choices we accept and understand. There are others that are much more important but don't get the same attention as the day-to-day choices. Being happy is one of those choices. Yes, you can choose to be happy. In *The 7 Habits of Highly Effective People*, Stephen Covey states that there is a gap between every stimulus and response, and our contentment often depends on how we choose to respond to a given stimulus.[4] We choose to be angry, we choose to be mad, and we can also choose to be happy. Marianne Williamson in her book, *A Return to*

Love, says, "The key to happiness is the decision to be happy…It is not only our right, but in a way our responsibility to be happy."[5]

At first, choosing to be happy wasn't the issue. I had thought I made that choice a long time ago and kept waiting and wondering when it would happen. It was as if my life was spent doing all that I thought was right, and being happy would be a consequence of choosing the right. Certainly, choosing the right had very positive consequences that I benefited from. For the most part, my conscious was clear, I felt I had integrity and was honest in my dealings with others, and I tried my best to be a good husband and father. Can't we all expect that choosing the right will bring us happiness and peace? So here was my dilemma: I was living a good life, and yet I was not happy, even after having a real desire to be happy. Of course, if I wasn't happy even after making the decision to be happy and choosing the right as best I could, then I must have done something wrong. It was so easy to blame everyone around me and my circumstances for my inability to be happy. Once I started looking, I found so many excuses for why I was not happy. My friend Joe helped me to see that the problem was not outside of me but inside of me. His advice was that *I* needed to be the change I wanted to see and that I really hadn't made the choice to be happy. Maybe I had made the choice on an intellectual level but not on an emotional level. He suggested that I focus more on the journey rather than the goal. Stephen Covey uses an example of having the right destination but the wrong map that I would like to borrow here. I had the right destination in mind, an important and wonderful destination—to be happy—but I was using the wrong map. It was as if I wanted to get to Southern California but entered Chicago into my navigation system.

The Happiness Factor is a map, or better yet, a navigation system, that guides you on the journey to be happy and living happily. I ask you to consider a few things to get started: (1) living happily is in the realm of possibilities for you and (2) happiness is a choice you can make. If you find it hard to comprehend those two things, take some time to ponder and consider the impact these two things can have on your life. Maybe you are not ready to accept the great miracle of living a satisfying and fulfilling life; maybe you need more time. If you are skeptical, try this small exercise: tomorrow when you wake up say to your self, "Today I choose to be happy no matter what." Say it several times to yourself with real intent. Write it down and think about it as your purpose for just one day. Visualize yourself seeing only the positive aspects of any situation. Make this a priority for just a single day. You will be surprised at the result. In essence, this simple choice, even for one day, will make a significant difference. Consider making it a habit, and imagine having a similar experience everyday for the rest of your life but at a magnitude that is much greater. It can happen!

The Happiness Factor

The Happiness Factor is set of principles that will help you develop a new mindset and the skills to dissolve adversity and negativity; a mindset of happiness that can be practiced and maintained. It starts with making the decision to be happy. The Happiness Factor is not a way to sugarcoat what happens to you but a set of real and powerful principles that provide the skills to be happy regardless of the situation or circumstance. Once you learn the Happiness Factor, you will attract peace and happiness into your life. The Happiness Factor becomes actionable for you by putting it together in an unforgettable and easy way that you can apply immediately and use often. I call this the P·E·A·S·E·F·U·L approach. It is a framework for the principles of the Happiness Factor, making it easy to remember and apply. (Yes, the S is deliberate). You use the framework this way: whenever you feel stress, worry, concern, or urgency, whenever you are experiencing negativity, adversity, or pain, you simply say, "I choose to be P•E•A•S•E•F•U•L," and then you apply the principles of the Happiness Factor.

The Happiness Factor

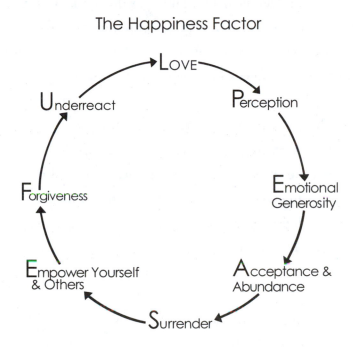

The Happiness Factor should be considered more of a continuum rather than a step-by-step approach. For convenience, this chapter will give an overview of the elements of P•E•A•S•E•F•U•L, and the chapters that follow will discuss each element individually. Chapter 2 discusses the first element, P (Perception), and the ninth chapter covers the final element, L (Love). Situations may call for love, and others may require you to change your mind or change your perception in order to become happy and restore peace. Regardless of the situation, regardless of the circumstances, you can always apply the Happiness Factor to bring peace and to be happy. I have had some clients say they use P•E•A•S•E•F•U•L to start their day. It allows them to recall the principles quickly and easily. You too can use this as a way to invite God to be your partner at the beginning of each day or at the end of the day as a way to review your daily experiences and learn valuable lessons. Using the Happiness Factor will dissolve anything that takes your peace and happiness away.

As you read this book, you will notice that I am not a psychologist nor trained as a counselor, I am just a guy—an average guy—and so I have endeavored to keep this in a conversational tone that is practical and actionable. This book purposely does not include a lot of scientific jargon nor does it purport to be a psychological journal. By necessity, most of the examples and experiences are from my own life, clients, coworkers, and friends because these are the experiences with which I am most familiar. Where appropriate I have replaced their names to protect their privacy. Additionally, you will find a natural overlap and integration of the various principles creating a slight repetition and intentional reinforcement of the topics. One very important note is that the Happiness Factor is not a checklist as much as it is a framework to be happy no matter what. It relates things that you should incorporate into your daily life, for it is in the "becoming" not the "doing" that you will be happy. The final chapter puts everything together in an easy to remember quick reference for the Happiness Factor using the P·E·A·S·E·F·U·L framework. I urge you to read on, to believe you can be happy no matter what, and to put these principles in to action and be happy.

P is for Perception

Perception is reality. Our world, the one we experience each day is created by our perceptions. We don't see the world as it is, we see the world from our own point of view; we see the world as we are. How we see the world and how we see others is a significant determinant of our happiness. It is so easy to blame others for our circumstances or unhappiness when in reality the key to happiness is actually within our grasp. When we change our perception, we change our circumstances. The chapter on perception will help you recognize how your perception can be used as a principle to be happy.

E is for Emotional generosity

Emotional generosity is the quality of being kind, welcoming and understanding of people around you, in all of their limitations, imperfections, and flaws. Emotional generosity means that you give other human beings the benefit of the doubt, that you cut them some slack, and that you are slow to be harsh, condemning, or judgmental. Emotional generosity is the greatest act of generosity you can offer, because it is an offering that only you can give, it is giving something of whom you are, not of what you have.

A is for Accepting what is and for Abundance

Accepting what is and abundance are two important principles of the Happiness Factor. Acceptance does not mean agreement. You can accept something or someone without agreeing with them. Acceptance is a way to get past denial and into action. So often we try to understand things we can't understand, which keeps us in denial. We also need to live in real time, neither in the past nor in the future. Abundance is the mindset that there is plenty for everyone. Abundance is an escape from greed, jealousy, and envy to a more peaceful mindset of gratitude. In the chapter on abundance, you will learn how to achieve abundance in four steps.

S is for Surrender

Surrender to win. It is a paradox that is difficult to understand at first. But the more you realize that all your worry and anxiety is wasted energy and that there is a higher power that loves you and is willing to be your partner, the more you can tap into the power of surrender. Surrendering is giving up on results, no longer prescribing the outcome, and letting go of control and manipulation. Surrendering your fears, relationships, problems, and adversity to be taken care of by your higher power, your God, allows you to live a problem- and worry-free life. It literally dissolves adversity and negativity.

E is for Empowering yourself and others to be happy

There may be a tendency to think that all we have to do is give our worries, problems, and adversity to God and sit back and watch him do all the work. The truth is that as we do our part, God will do his part. Our part may require us to do things that are hard, things that are outside our comfort zone. The difference is that we now have the ultimate partner in doing those things. Our part is to live a wholesome life full of integrity, making and keeping promises, and being true to ourselves. Doing all we can with love, compassion, and kindness empowers us to be happy. At the same time, our happiness, our kindness, compassion, and love empower those around you to be happy as well.

F is for Forgiveness

Every offense that has occurred in the past only has life as long as it lives on in your memory. To a certain degree, when we hold a grudge, we are holding on to the past and letting it control our emotions and thinking. The ego needs to hold grudges as a survival tactic, convincing us that we are more important than others. Self-importance is a myth, because we are all equally important. Forgiveness will bring you unimaginable peace and confidence. Your mind will become clear, you will be able to love more deeply, and you will be happy.

U is for Underreact

"I choose to underreact," is a very powerful statement and choice in any situation and circumstance. We all have a tendency to overreact, and it is understandable that we overreact in situations that are serious and warrant our attention. But many of us also overreact to circumstances that are not so important. Developing the skill of underreacting can bring you enormous peace and allow you to see solutions to your problems that you simply could not see before. Choosing to underreact is choosing peace and love over anything else.

L is for Love

Love is all that is real. Anything else is an illusion. Any action or response is either love or a cry for love. We either operate from a fear-centric position or a love-centric position. Love brings with it the power to dissolve all negativity and conflict. God's will in any situation is to simply and purposefully love. When we stray from love, we feel jealousy, envy, strife, and contention. Love attracts kindness, security, peace, and affection and is activated by giving it away and extending it into any situation. Often we think of love as a feeling between two or more people. But it is more than that; love is energy and has the power to transform a situation and your circumstances.

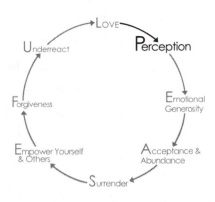

Chapter 2
Perception

The key to being happy lies within you and begins with how you perceive what happens to you.

Most of the obstacles we experience are the results of our own thinking—our mindset. In many cases, we are our own worst enemy. We all accept that if we eat healthy food, we will have better health and if we eat junk food, we will have poor health. The same analogy is true for our thought process as well. Faulty and biased thought patterns will result in faulty or biased experiences. It is our own thought pattern, or mindset, that creates the framework by which we experience life. This framework is commonly called perception. What is seen as negativity and adversity is different for each person. The exact same circumstances will be experienced differently by each of us. What is seen as an opportunity by one is seen as adversity for another. So varied are the individual responses that the circumstance itself cannot be the determinate factor of your own peace and happiness. Contrary to popular belief, circumstances are neutral, neither positive nor negative. Contentedness and happiness are derived from our perception, and our perception is created by our own thoughts. The Buddha is quoted as saying, "Our life is shaped by our mind; we become what we think. Joy s a pure thought like a shadow that never leaves."[6] We think what we choose to think. The gift to think for ourselves is the greatest gift given to man. The key to being happy lies within you and begins with how you perceive what happens to you.

It is a common mistake to believe that what and how we see people, events, and circumstances create our response and feelings. In actuality, it is the reverse. Our thoughts are the source of our feelings and create our experience. Because thoughts are voluntary, we can change what we experience by realizing that what we think is not necessarily reality. Thoughts are often random and arbitrary. There has been a lot of literature over the years on the effects of positive thinking. Without a doubt, positive thinking is important in the pursuit of happiness. Much of the positive-thinking literature promotes a mind-control approach, teaching you to control your thoughts to only be positive. That kind of control is impossible. Trying to achieve it will create a constant battle in your mind between your negative and positive thoughts. Happy people have both negative thoughts and positive thoughts. The difference is that rather than trying to control their thoughts, happy people learn to not give heed to negative thoughts because their happiness and peace have a higher priority. Happy people dismiss negative thinking as if it were a scary movie. Scary movies are enjoyable because they are not real, which is why people say, "It's only a movie." This is true of negative thoughts as well. They are not reality, and when you consider that they are not real, the negative thoughts are easier to dismiss.

We see things differently when we have positive thoughts than when we have negative thoughts, and so our experience is not based on the circumstances but on how we perceive them. Negative thoughts and negative thought patterns actually distort reality, causing us to perceive the world as being more hostile than it actually is. Our feelings and moods are a result of this thought framework, not a result of our circumstances and of what happens to us. If we allow it, negative thought patterns will cause us to draw an unjustified and incorrect conclusion. For instance, Jack has been working late explaining to his wife he needs to stay at the office to work on a big project. Jack has never had to stay late before, and so this upsets his wife as she considers that he is lying to her. Her thoughts lead her down a path to think that he is having an affair, and she neglects other possible explanations.

Another negative thought pattern happens when we focus our attention on one singular detail without regard to the rest. For example, Theresa is upset that she has a poor complexion. She feels that no boy will look at her unless her skin is clear. She does not consider that she has other wonderful and beautiful assets such as being musically gifted and smart. To her, those things are of little importance.

Perhaps we have the habit of over generalizing and drawing conclusions based on little information. Sarah, for instance, just discovered her teenage daughter has been drinking. She is naturally distraught and concludes that it must be the influence of her friends. She concludes that her daughter must be taking drugs as well. Her thoughts lead her to believe that her daughter is no longer trustworthy and requires much closer supervision. Sarah neglects to take into account that this could be experimentation, not addiction. I am not suggesting that she ignore the event, but that she approach it from a learning stance rather than arriving at a conclusion without more information.

Another dangerous and faulty thought pattern is magnification or exaggeration, commonly known as "freaking out." Getting a traffic ticket is unpleasant and perhaps embarrassing but not the end of the world. To some it is a devastating experience. Others will simply accept that they need to drive slower or more safely and move on. Our thought framework, our perception, can either work for us by creating a positive and happy experience or against us by creating a negative experience. The choice is yours.

It's all about you!

After reading the previous pages you might say, "I get that happiness is a choice—but this guy hasn't met my mother-in-law!" You're right! I haven't met your mother-in-law, or your husband, your children, your mother, your boss, or your coworker. Nor have I met the person that cut you off in traffic this morning or the boss who criticizes your work and never acknowledges your accomplishments. Though I have not met them, I know of them and would recognize them in a heartbeat. These are the people that most of us blame for our own unhappiness. Just listen to the people around you at church, at the gym, at your child's back-to-school night, and you will quickly learn that as a whole we are experts at blaming others. We spend a lifetime waiting for those around us to change into something that will bring us happiness, but it will *never* happen. No one can change enough to bring you happiness, because happiness is found on the inside, not on the outside. *Happiness is not about anyone else. It's all about you!*

If you are one of those people expecting others to change so that you can be happy, your wait is in vain. It cannot and will not happen. You don't need to feel hopeless, because it is not about them, it's all about you. You don't need to wait for anyone else to change for you to be happy! This may be a hard thing to accept because it strips you of all the excuses and blame you have used for years. When excuses and pretense are stripped away, you have to take responsibility and accountability for your own life and your own level of satisfaction. To some this will be scary, while for others, this will be an enabling and powerful concept. Your peace, your satisfaction, your happiness is up to you. In the next sections, you will find out how to take charge of the power that creates happiness. Let's explore a few subjects that will unleash this pow

set a foundation for becoming happy. Remember, it is not about anyone

else; it's all about you!

Crabs in a bucket

What is it about fairy tales that captures our hearts and imagination? As children we are captivated by the magic of fairy tales that have been told over and over for generations. When my daughter was young, we were engrossed by the new wave of films such as *The Little Mermaid* and *The Lion King*, which we watched over and over until the VHS tape wore out. Why is that? What is it about those stories that appeal to us? For me it is the story of something ordinary transforming into the extraordinary. It is not just fairy tales either. Stories about Spider-Man and Indiana Jones, where the most common of men become heroes and reach extraordinary heights, interest and inspire me. But what about the rest of us? Can just plain people like you and me reach extraordinary heights and do amazing things? The answer is a resounding yes! But why don't we? Because we have been trained to limit ourselves and put a limit on our own satisfaction. Just when you feel the excitement of doing something fantastic, a small voice within you tells you all the reasons why you can't do it. That voice, a voice we all hear and contend with, is the combined voices of people you have encountered over the years that have trained and taught you that fairy tales are fiction, that miracles portrayed in simple stories don't come true. This is sometimes referred to as the "crab bucket syndrome." It is said that if you want to keep a live crab in a bucket, put more than one crab in it. As one crab tries to climb out of the bucket, the other crab will pull it down. We are like crabs in a bucket! As soon as we try to climb out, there is always someone trying to pull us back down. In our youth, we approach the world with awe and wonder, thinking that anything is possible. We think by simply wishing hard enough and trying hard enough anything is possible. We grow up sadly disappointed that the things we once thought possible now seem impossible. How do we know things are impossible? Again, just ask the people around you. For every wonderful idea you have, there are tens to hundreds of people out there to tell you why it is impossible. They can enumerate all the reasons why your dreams cannot come true. We are surrounded by naysayers that speak with such conviction and apparent knowledge that it is hard to persevere and maintain grand thoughts and ideals. In this case, the adage that misery loves company is evident as people try to bring us down, thinking that if they can't have happiness or great ideas, then no one can. They may not do this intentionally; it is the way they too have been trained. As we become more mature, the magic we once felt in our youth is replaced by apathy, wonder is replaced by skepticism, and we become blind to the miracles that happen around us each day. The result is that we end up only seeing what we don't have instead of what is possible. We only see the lack in our lives. You don't have to live that way. There are miracles around you; all you need to do is open your eyes and see them. You can reach new heights by learning not to listen to the voices you hear that limit your potential and achievements. Use selective hearing. We all listen to what we want to listen to. The trick here is to grow in your desire to only pay attention to positive affirmations instead of negative. There is another voice inside you, and with practice you will find that it speaks louder than you think. It is the voice of your divine nature, the Holy Spirit; it is a voice full of kindness, compassion, love, and service.

This chapter is devoted to helping you capture the wonder back into your world by changing your perception from one of negativity and criticism to a mindset of being happy. Find that sense of awe and wonder that heightens your senses, opens your eyes to beauty, and unfolds the mystery of being happy.

The Holy Spirit and the ego

You have heard it said that first impressions are the hardest to break or that first impressions last the longest. It is true; we all make first impressions of the people we meet based on our perception.

I love to people-watch. Spending a lot of time in airports you see a lot of people, and it is hard not to wonder what their story is. Where they are going? What do they do? Even without meeting someone, you can have an impression of them based on mostly superficial appearances. Have you ever encountered someone for the first time and their ego is so strong and pervasive that you have a hard time actually "meeting" them. You are too busy contending with their ego, as if it were some sort of force field keeping you from getting to know them. Everyone has an ego; some even have an alter-ego.

Someone has said that if you say you don't have an ego, you do, and if you say you do, then you do. However, I am referring to the ego in the way the Greeks defined it, not the popular definition as simply arrogance and pride. The Greeks defined the ego as a separate and distinct "self" within us, a "self" separate from our divine nature. We weren't born with an ego; we *learned* it. We developed it over years and years of training. We are born into a state of innocence and purity, full of love and unable to discern right from wrong until we reach an age of accountability. Accountability comes after a lot of teaching and training.

I was born to some well-intended parents that wanted the best for me and did their best to teach me how to be successful. Even with the best of intentions, we inherit many of our parents' philosophies and traits—traits you may or may not agree with. Just living life itself is a great teacher. We are taught to be competitive, to strive for first place, to compare ourselves to others. We learn what it means and how it feels to win and to lose. We learn through very powerful means that winners get more attention than losers. We learn that beautiful people are treated differently and that people with college degrees earn more and are happier. Just look around and you will see that we have learned that success is defined by accumulation.

With all of these powerful lessons, we forget the divine nature we are born with. It is our divine nature that defines us as a creation of God. This divine nature is what should define success, not the ego. As we grow up, mature, and start listening to the people around us more than listening to the Holy Spirit, our ego becomes stronger to a point where we become separated from God—only to spend a lifetime trying to reunite with him. It is this separation that strengthens the ego to the point where we think we *are* the ego. We become so identified with *things* that we forget who we truly *are*. We become what we do or what we possess. The ego wants to convince us that our divine nature is fiction and that the meaning of life is found in material things, not within our hearts and minds. The mission of the ego is to separate us from our divine nature, thus separating us from God. God is love, and so the ego's mission is to separate us from love. When we can accept our divine nature as a creation of God, we learn to define our true success.

God's answer to the ego is the Holy Ghost, the Holy Spirit, the Spirit of God, or your maker. Regardless of your belief system the ego is in opposition to it. Let me take a few minutes to further describe the ego. As I do, consider how this is evident in your life and also consider if this leads you to happiness or discontent.

The ego looks out for you as number one by teaching selfishness, greed, judgment, and blame. The ego uses loud laughter, evil speaking, and light-mindedness as its methods. It has extreme magnetism attracting to it all that is negative, creating barriers to feeling the Holy Spirit.

The ego teaches you that you don't need anyone else or anything else to feel content or happy. It insists on being right; it holds grudges and seeks vengeance; it is easily offended. The ego finds it hard to forgive and causes you to overreact. The ego's wants are never ending. It convinces us that we are unworthy, not good enough, ugly, and incompetent.

Another aspect of the ego is that its perception is based in the past and carries that perception into the present and the future, recreating the past into a never-ending cycle of worldliness and despair. It creates worry, anxiety, and depression by focusing on what we don't have or what we need to live up to instead of being grateful for what we have. Marianne Williamson, in her book *A Return to Love*, makes this observation of the ego: "The ego says that we can project our anger onto another person and not feel it ourselves."[7] She goes on to say that whatever we project onto another we feel ourselves. The ego is the master of lies and is so good at lying that we believe it. We believe the ego when it creates masterful excuses. One of the boldest lies of the ego is that we are not worthy or we are incapable of happiness, that because of some event in the past or some character flaw we inherited from our parents, we cannot and will not be happy. The ego is the great saboteur—as we approach happiness and peace, the ego will do anything to convince us otherwise. How often have you heard someone say, "Just when I thought I would find happiness, something happens and I am sadder than before"? That is the ego convincing you that you are unable to be happy. These are just lies, and you need to recognize them as lies.

The ego is the great destroyer of relationships. When we demand or expect others to be the way we want them to be, even under the guise of creating a "good" relationship, it is our demand and need for control that comes from the ego. The ego creates its own agenda for every relationship and convinces you to leave the relationship if you don't get what you want when you want it. In every encounter, in every relationship, we either lead with the ego or with our divine nature. The ego wants control; the Holy Spirit wants to love. It is up to you to decide which will have force in your life.

The opposite of the ego is divine nature. This is who we really are. We are not our ego; we are the embryo of a God. Is an acorn an oak? An acorn has oak DNA just as we have the DNA of God; we may not be a God, but at our core—if we examine our truest selves—we are divine. It is through the teaching of well-minded people and our acceptance of the ego that we have forgotten who we really are. Our divine nature was created and is delivered by the Holy Spirit. The Holy Spirit teaches love instead of hate, to be kind, to be grateful, and tolerant. The Holy Spirit is slow to anger, does not take offense, and is full of compassion. The Holy Spirit is what enables us to develop the attributes of divine nature, to make divine choices. It is our divine nature that rejoins us with God to be one with him in all we do. Not long ago, there was a popular saying among Christians, "What would Jesus do?" and even the acronym WWJD. We can rediscover our divine nature so we do what Jesus would do automatically; it becomes who we are not just what we would do. Rediscovering our divine nature is the whole point of Marianne William's book *A Return to Love*. Her premise is that God is love, and so as we return—rejoin—with God, we are returning to who we really are. We are God's, and to be his is to love and to have divine nature. When I first considered this, it seemed almost too good to be true, too incredible to believe, but the more I contemplated that I am God's and I am his to love, the more it became real to me.

If the ego is so strong and powerful, how can anyone rise above it and focus on their divine nature? As I said before, I wasn't a bad guy. Looking back, I think I was in pretty good shape with God and my fellow man. But there was something missing. There was a constant battle between the ego and my divine nature. The ego convinced me that things were so bad that I needed to take terrible and severe action. However, I learned that I would never become happy without first shedding myself of the ego and establishing my divine nature as my *default* nature. The ego will control and manipulate your life unless you accept that the ego is powerful; accept that it is a real force in your life and ask God for the miracle of letting the Holy Spirit be the prominent force in your life. When my wife and I were first married, we had a visitor come and stay with us. He was to stay just a few weeks. When it turned into months, I had to do something I didn't want to do. I had to ask him to leave. I liked this person and enjoyed his company and conversation. He was not imposing as much as he was preventing my wife and me from growing together and bettering ourselves. It is the same with the ego. You like the ego, it brings you pleasure, it builds you up and makes you feel important. But that's empty flattery. With God's help, you can turn from the ego and return to God. Without God's help, you can make progress, but it will be by "brute force." That is how I would describe my attempts at happiness before I realized the miracle of the Happiness Factor. It was a brute-force mentality. It was a constant battle between the ego and the Holy Spirit. However, by recognizing my divine nature, letting it grow within me, surrendering to God, and accepting his help, I have found that a transformation can take place through the grace and miracles of God. It was up to me; it is up to you.

The ego is an enemy to God in the fullest sense because it denies the magic of miracles and demands evidence for the unseen. Not only is the ego an enemy to God, it is an enemy to all that is good. I have met many good-hearted people that are miserable because they have allowed the ego to control their life. You can free yourself from your ego. It is a *huge* and necessary step toward being happy.

The ego will fight against the ideas that I am presenting because they are a departure from the habits you have formed. You can develop the habit of being happy. Dr. David D. Ireland writes, "The habits of happy people are intentional responses that have proven to meet their need to manage life. These happy people did not start out knowing that habits that would bring them happiness; rather, they learned these responses along the way to a satisfying life."[8] These habits are yours to learn.

The miracle of a changed mind

The ego that I have described is in your mind. It is *all* in your mind. Think of all that I said about the ego: it's vengeful, easily offended, quick to anger, and unable to forgive, it's all in your mind. Think of something someone did to hurt your feelings—it is all in your mind. Maybe it is something your father said—it is all in your mind. Something you mother did when you were young that you have remembered and held on to—it is all in your mind. When I first learned this concept, it was hard for me to accept because I thought it minimized the event. It doesn't minimize it. It is a fact! All events that happened in the past and all events that will happen in the future do not exist. They only have life in your mind. To change your experience, you simply need to change your mind, to think of the event differently. The beauty is that as you change your mind about the past, it changes your present and current experience. To rid yourself of the ego is to change your mind.

When Adam and Eve were placed in the garden, they lived in bliss and harmony. The Bible says, "They walked with God." In their innocence, they were with God, and he was with them. They were pure and innocent, and there was beauty all around them. They saw it and noticed it. One day, Eve met up with the serpent, and he convinced her that her life in the garden was superficial and not satisfying. He convinced her that she didn't know the sweet because she had never tasted the bitter. Together, Adam and Eve partook of the forbidden fruit. Where did that fruit come from? It was picked fresh off the Tree of *Knowledge* of good and evil. Once they partook of the fruit, their lives changed completely. For the first time, they saw they were naked, and the serpent told them to hide and cover themselves. It is important to note that for the most part their circumstances did not change. They were as naked before eating the fruit as they were after. The fruit was that of *knowledge*—knowledge exists in the mind. In essence, their minds changed—their minds changed in such a way that they saw themselves in a whole new light. They now had a new perspective, new knowledge, and because of this they experienced a separation from their divine nature as they were cast out of the Garden to toil and labor. Just like Adam and Eve, our perspective can separate us from God. I believe it is possible to bridge the gap, to overcome our separation from God. We can cultivate and learn the perspective of God and thus unite with him. To be happy you need to change your mind. Change from an ego-driven mindset to a mindset led by the Holy Spirit.

When I was in the sixth grade, I ran across a book in the library titled *The Brain*. This was not some cheesy Frankenstein story; this was a scientific book on the brain itself. I was fascinated with this book and kept it for several months despite the urging from my teacher to return the book to the library. This book explained that on a physiological level the brain does not know the difference between a lie and the truth. The author went on to explain that if you told yourself a lie long enough you would believe it as the truth. Though young and immature I decided to put this to the test. Not getting a lot of positive reinforcement at home I decided that I would "lie" by telling myself that I was a good person, that I had great talent, that I was smart and good-looking. Each night as I went to bed, I would pick a positive phrase and say it over and over to myself as I went to sleep. At first it was all lies! I was speaking lies to myself because what I heard every day was the opposite—not only from others around me but in my own mind as well. The ego had a loud voice telling me how bad I was, how stupid, how slow, how weird. In the beginning it felt awkward and foreign to say good things about myself, but after several days, the discomfort started to fade and I began to actually *believe* the lies. Soon that belief became truth, and I began to become what I was telling myself. I was becoming good, smart, good-looking, and talented. A significant and tremendous transformation took place that year. The boy that started the sixth grade was not the same boy that ended the sixth grade. My teacher, Mr. Woolsey, even noticed and gave me the "Most Outstanding Student" award. My experience in the sixth grade was a miracle; it was a *brute-force* method of changing my mind, bringing me greater peace and a greater ability to deal with the negativity around me as I changed my self-perception. I was too young then to understand what had happened, that I literally changed my mind. I have since learned a more elegant way to change my mind to find greater peace—a way that I want to share with you.

Just a few years ago I learned the same lesson, but it was more miraculous than before; I learned that I can turn to God and ask for the miracle of a changed mind, and it will happen. God has given us the greatest of gifts: the ability to think and choose for ourselves. We can think what we want to think. For better or worse, our minds are our own. If Satan had his way we would all think alike and be compelled to do what is right. We would be controlled and manipulated without any choice. The gift of choice, or agency, is given to man to think his own thoughts and decide for himself if he will follow the ego or the Holy Spirit. Because of this gift, God will not compel us in any way; he won't even compel us to believe in him. That too is up to us. God will not and cannot interfere with our thoughts unless we give him permission to do so. We can literally grant him permission to change our minds. If we desire to change our mind and to think of something differently, we need to ask for this miracle. We literally give God permission to change our mind and perspective and it will happen. When I was in fifth grade, I was shot in the thigh with an arrow. My brother and I were shooting arrows at each other—a dumb thing to do, and exactly what you think would happen, happened. I saw the arrow coming and could not move fast enough, so the arrow impaled my thigh. To tell our parents meant certain punishment, so I hid the wound. The wound festered and infected the rest of my leg. With medical intervention and prayers it was healed. Consider the ego as a mind-wound. Think of selfishness, hatred, the need for revenge, and any negative thought as a wound inside your mind and, like my thigh, in need of healing. Our negative thoughts, if not taken care of, will also infect the rest of our lives. So often it is our thoughts that bring us unhappiness and grief. God is the great healer. In this case, our mind is sick—sick with negative thoughts driven by the ego. Call upon God, ask for him to heal your mind, and you will be healed. You could say this: "God, I am willing to think of this differently. My mind is wounded. Will you heal my mind by helping me see this situation differently?" In his book, *The Power of Intention*, Dr. Wayne Dyer supports this when he says, "Change the way you look at things, and the things you look at change."[9] Problems, adversity and pain will be dissolved as you change your mind. Ask God to help you see with his eyes, to see things with Love. God said, "Ask and ye shall receive." When you ask this with real intent, he is bound to grant your request.

To make this point, let's consider an example. Quite recently I was in turmoil over something someone had said to me. I was offended and upset. I didn't want to be upset, but this person's words cut deeply, and I lost peace by obsessing over how mean and disrespectful this person had been. The actual event occurred several months in the past, and yet it lived on in my mind, causing me distress. I couldn't look at this person; I avoided him whenever I saw him. This event existed only in my mind. My mind was wounded and needed to be healed. Exactly like the wound caused by the arrow in my leg, the negative thoughts about this person festered and started to infect other aspects of my life. When I was hit with the arrow, my brother and I were afraid of getting help because it meant confessing the deed, confessing that we were doing something we should not have been. It wasn't until my mother saw me limping and the blood stain on my pants that I got the help I needed. I finally had to admit I needed help, that I was wounded and needed to be healed. Was it painful? Yes, but only because I didn't take care of it sooner. The longer I waited, the worse it got. The same is true with negative events that live on in our mind: the longer we wait, the worse it gets.

Don't think that just because the event happened long ago that you don't need to take care of it. Step one: be willing to think of the event and the person differently. Step two: ask God to change your mind. To help me, I spoke a simple yet powerful prayer that went like this: "Father, I have been hurt. My mind is wounded. I am willing to think of this event and this person differently. Will you please heal my mind? I give you permission to cause me to forget the event and help me have compassion for this person and to think of them as child of God. To only see good in them. To see them as someone that you love." For several days this was my prayer, and each day my mind began to heal. I no longer had the emotion associated with this event, and eventually I forgot about it until I needed to conjure it up to include in this book. This was nothing less than a miracle. I was returned to peace, I was able to once again feel happiness, and I was able to look this person in the eye and feel whole once again. I am not so special. If you want to be happy, you must learn to recognize when your mind is wounded and needs to be healed from the wounds caused by the ego. This is hard because holding on to wounds sometimes feels so good. Learn to give God permission to change your mind. You see, the circumstances did not change—my mind changed. The person I was mad at did not change; they didn't need to change. This literally had nothing to do with the other person. My mind changed, and my life changed. It was *all* about me. The event resided in my mind; it only had life in my mind, and when my mind changed, the event disappeared.

Several years ago my wife encountered a dog that had been hit by a car. Motorists were passing by, but no one was stopping to help. My wife stopped to help, and as she approached the dog, she was attacked. Our minds act similarly—when we are wounded we want to attack, we want revenge. That is the ego talking. Step back; be willing to consider that this is all up to you. You can have peace if you want to, and that peace comes from surrendering your thoughts to God and letting him heal you. Like me, many of you have tried to do this on your own and failed. You don't need to use a brute-force method any longer. Becoming happy is healing your mind by asking God to change it.

Self justification and resentment

There is another aspect to the ego that stands as a barrier to being happy. The ego is obsessed with being right. Now, you may not think you have the need to be right all the time, and you may even be one of the rare individuals that are able to admit when you are wrong. Nevertheless, there is a strong impulse for the ego to be justified in being right. There have been many books written on this subject, and my favorite is a small book written by Terry Warner of the Arbinger Institute entitled *Leadership and Self Deception*. I highly recommend this book. Not only is it powerful and compelling, it is written in a way that is easy to understand and internalize. Self-deception and resentment follow the law of the harvest applied to our thoughts. We all know of the law of the harvest as expressed in the Bible. The apostle Paul enunciated the law of the harvest when he declared that "whatsoever a man soweth, that shall he also reap." (Gal. 6:7) It is true in life with our actions as it is with our thoughts. In fact, it may be even truer with our thoughts. Negative thoughts will reap negative consequences. Positive thoughts result in positive consequences. It really is as simple as it sounds. However, you may be so used to your own way of thinking that you do not recognize it for what it is. You may be thinking that bad things don't happen to you, so how can negative thoughts result in negative consequences. The most common negative consequence is a lack of peace that prevents you from being happy. Another consequence is resentment and self-deception.[10]

Consider this as an example. Suppose your husband leaves his dirty clothes lying on the floor. You don't like picking up his dirty clothes, and you don't understand why it is so hard to put them in the hamper where they belong. You might even say to yourself, "He is so lazy. Doesn't he realize that I have enough to do already without having to clean up after him?" Your thoughts may be followed with, "What a slob." This is the ego talking. At first blush you might consider it innocent and think that it wouldn't cause any harm. Besides, who would know you were thinking that anyway? What harm could a simple thought do? However, each time you pick up his dirty clothes, you are doing it with resentment toward him, and before long, the ego will demand justification for the negative thoughts by finding all that is wrong with him—this is the ego justifying itself. If left unchecked, all possible evidence of laziness, inconsideration, and disrespect in your spouse will be found. Resentment feeds the ego; it gives power and enablement to build a case against someone, to find fault, to criticize, and to do it in a way that has no escape but to feed the ego with more power. This goes back to the concept of "seek and ye shall find." Self-justification finds what the ego is looking for. The ego is an expert at self-justification that leads to resentment. Where there is resentment there cannot be love. Where there is not love there cannot be peace. In this example, you need to ask for the miracle of a changed mind and also ask to replace the negative thoughts with thoughts of compassion that lead to love and understanding. I would suggest saying a simple prayer expressing that you are willing to look at this situation with complete kindness and compassion—that you are willing to consider that perhaps your spouse has a lot on his mind, maybe he is distracted and picking up the clothes is a way of serving him. As you then pick up the clothes your thoughts are not resentful but compassionate. The same act went from a vengeful act to an act of service and kindness, and acts of service and kindness are also part of the law of the harvest. These acts will reap positive consequences in a greater peace of mind and the ability to be happy. Again I point out that the circumstances did not change. The clothes did not magically pick themselves up, nor did your spouse transform overnight. The only thing that changed was your own mind preventing the ego from self-justification.

Resentment, if left unchecked, will contaminate a relationship and work like a cancer that slowly eats away at your peace and your well-being. I have seen resentment destroy families, lead to divorce, and keep parents and children from speaking for years and years. Resentment fuels the ego, and learning to recognize it and dissolve it will bring you peace and empower you to be happy. I have met many people who resist the idea that they resent the people around them. Resentment has a strong negative connotation. If someone were to say, "I resent you," he or she would be expressing a strong emotion. I have found a simple and accurate test to determine if you have resentment toward someone. If you ever hear yourself say, "John is such a jerk," or "Susan always does this," or "Every time I try to be nice to my mom she just shoves it in my face," it is evident that you resent the other person, which gives the ego all the ammunition it needs to justify itself by finding all that is wrong with them. Resentment is only in your mind, and you can remove it by asking God to change your mind.

As a man thinketh—so you are.

Proverbs 23:7 has a powerful message, "For as he thinketh in his heart, so is he…" I believe that scripture to be true but would like to turn it around a bit: "as a man thinketh, so you are." Our thoughts are a form of energy that has an impact on the world and the people around us. Low energy or vibration is created by negative thoughts while positive thoughts produce higher energy waves. This was proven by Dr. Masaru Emoto of Japan. Several years ago, he took river water and looked at it microscopically when frozen and found that it was dirty and unorganized. He then wrote several positive statements on paper and taped them to the outside of the jar containing the river water. These sayings were "thank you," "I love you," and similar words that we would all consider positive. After several days he examined the water again and found that it had begun to form organized crystals. The experiment was repeated several times with the same results. He did the same test with negative phrases and found that the frozen water was dirtier and in chaos. The words themselves, expressing positive or negative thoughts, had a measurable impact on the water.[11] The human body consists of mostly water. Consider the impact your thoughts are having on your body and the bodies of those around you. David Hawkins's book *Power versus Force: The Hidden Determinants of Human Behavior* interprets empirical data from studies conducted over many years and demonstrates that thoughts are energy and have an impact on your surroundings.[12] Thus my quote above, "as a man thinketh, so you are." Or "my thoughts about you are what you will be." If I have negative thoughts about you, not only does the ego fight hard for self-justification, the resentment and negativity of my thoughts has a physical impact on you! Imagine the significance of this in your daily life. If you are a doctor, having positive healing thoughts can help your patients heal. The opposite is also true: if as a doctor you have disdain for your patients and think of them as a bother and a nuisance, it cou them and slow the healing process.

Most of us are not doctors, but we find ourselves every day in circumstances where projecting positive thoughts can have a tremendous impact on the situation. Not long ago I was attempting to return a rather expensive piece of electronics to a store with a very strict return policy of no returns without a receipt after thirty-days. I did not have the receipt, and it was well over thirty days. I am sure you have been in similar situations, and you know how hard it would be to keep a positive frame of mind. I put this to the test. From the time I left my home to the time I stood in front of the customer service desk, I was projecting love and kindness to whoever would help me. I was upfront with her and told her the product was purchased several months ago and that I did not have a receipt. She was pleasant and helpful and gave me the refund I wanted. Surely she did not do anything wrong, and it would have been understandable if she had said no. This was a small miracle that benefited me, and I attribute it to the positive thoughts of love and kindness that I was projecting. They had a physical impact on the situation. You attract into your life what you think about and dwell upon. In the example above, I attracted into my life benefits from dwelling upon kindness and love. I know for a fact that if I had been projecting negative thoughts and demanding a refund for whatever reason, the situation would have escalated. I might have still got the refund, but only after badgering the manager and losing peace over it. Believe me, the refund was not worth losing peace over.

We are constantly communicating. Regardless of whether we are speaking or not, we are communicating implied messages created by what we are thinking. No matter how hard you try, you cannot conceal what you are actually thinking. It is not that others can read your thoughts, per say, but they get the message. I am sure you have all experienced this at one time or another as evidenced by miscommunication. This miscommunication happens because the implied message is more powerful than the spoken words. There are some people whom I interact with whose implied messages are so powerful that I cannot hear and understand what they are saying. For instance, you compliment your son for cleaning his room without being told, but at the same time you are thinking, "What does he want?" or "Why can't he keep his room clean like that all the time?" Regardless of how hard you try to say the right thing, your thoughts create an implied message that is communicated at a different level, and the compliment loses its intended effect. If you want to communicate truthfully and clearly, you must first start with your own thoughts and perspective. You must communicate from the inside out. I have tried this with great success. Many times in business I have had to work with and communicate with someone I really didn't like. No matter how hard I tried, the communication was stressed and unpleasant and resulted in several escalations and issues because we misunderstood each other. That typically does not happen between friends. When you like someone, when you have positive feelings, thoughts, and ideas about another person, the communication is not stressed, it is more clear and understood. Why? Because the implied messages now match the verbal messages; the inside matches the outside. Whenever I have a coaching client who complains about their spouse or a coworker, I ask them to delve into how they perceive this person. I ask them whether they like this person or not and to pay attention to how many negative things they say versus how many positive things they say. It is a simple test—if there are more negative comments, chances are the relationship is strained. As I help them learn to only consider the positive traits of a spouse or coworker, the relationship almost always becomes less strained, and peace returns. Your relationships stem from the inside out. I have experienced this with my children and my wife.

The more positive my thoughts and ideas about them, the better we communicate, and the greater peace comes into our relationship. As a man thinketh so you are!

Another aspect of this is found in the original proverb, "As a man thinketh, so is he." If you think about how poor you are, you will attract poverty into your life regardless of how much money you make. If you think about what a terrible job you have, your job will be terrible and may even get worse. Our thoughts are magnetic; they have intense gravitational pull. You no doubt have heard the phrase "misery loves company." It is not just true on an emotional level; it is also true on a metaphysical level. If you can think of positive outcomes, such as making more money or having a great job, you will attract that into your life. By visualizing yourself in the place you want to be, feeling what you want to feel, being what you want to be, your mind and your intent synchronize, and the doors needed to make it happen will open. What I am describing is habit 2 in the bestselling book *7 Habits of Highly Effective People*, where Stephen Covey describes the power of "starting with the end in mind." He says, "To begin with the end in mind means to start with a clear understanding of your destination. It means to know where you're going so that you better understand where you are now and so that the steps you take are always in the right direction."[13] Our daily thoughts create a map that we live by, and most of the time we have no idea where we are headed. The more we can see our destination in our mind and actually put ourselves in that situation, feeling what we want to feel, the more likely it is to happen.

After my experience in the sixth grade learning how to change my mind, I became quite convinced that positive thinking can bring great success. Over and over again I practiced positive thoughts with marginal success. Visualization is more than positive thinking; it is an actual visualization that you create with the end in mind and then backing up in time to understand what it takes to get there. In essence, you are doing what Stephen Covey speaks about in his book. Instead of traveling along the default script created by your random thoughts, you are creating a map of how to achieve your goals. My goal was to be happy, to lead a satisfied life regardless of the situation. I started by first visualizing myself with a smile and happy feelings, and almost without really understanding how and why it happened, more people began smiling at me, and I felt brighter and had a more positive attitude. I was able to handle setbacks and contention much better. How we see ourselves makes a tremendous difference in our level of satisfaction. Dream for a minute about what it would feel like to be happy, to live happily ever after. Create that picture in your mind and revisit it and grow upon it regularly. Rather than living your life by default, live your life with purpose and with a vision. "We reactively live the scripts handed to us by family, associates, other people's agendas, the pressures of circumstance—scripts from our earlier years, from our training, our conditioning. The unique human capacities of self-awareness, imagination and conscience enable us to…write our own script," Covey says.[14] Visualize living a satisfied life, and it is more likely to happen. In subsequent chapters, I will expand on this and give specific examples of how and what to visualize to attract happiness and abundance into your life. When you couple visualization with real intent, you will be amazed at the results. It will be no less than miraculous.

Becoming happy is all about you and up to you. No one can make you happy; no thing can make you happy. It is all about you. But not about you in the sense that you stand alone against the world and all that is wrong. Your maker, your God will help you. You can start by recognizing the ego, its effect on your life, and how it destroys peace and prevents you from living happily. You are not your ego. You are a child version of God, a child of God; you have divine nature. This divine nature has been lying dormant since you became separated from God by the ego. It is there; it will always be there. Darth Vader in Star Wars allowed the ego to take over his mind, and in the end, his divine nature started to awaken. Don't wait for a crisis in your life to awaken your divine nature. There are so many stories of people who have needed to "hit rock bottom" before transforming their lives. Maybe you will need that level of despair before you learn to be happy. However, it is not a requirement. Call upon God, and with his help, you can change your mind to see the world around you differently. As you do, you will awaken your divine nature and approach life with love and kindness and bring unlimited peace into your life. You can be happy. It is all about you!

The power of perspective

Everyone who has ever traveled by airplane knows that the middle seat is the worst seat on the plane. No one likes the middle seat; it is last on anyone's list of favorite seats. Yet, there are times when the middle seat *is* the best seat on the plane! Can you think of when that is? I will tell you. Just three years ago, I was traveling in Europe on business and happened to be in Italy when my mobile phone rang. It was my father's number on the caller ID, and it was only 5:00 a.m. in Boise, Idaho, where he lived. Immediately, I knew it was bad news. Sure enough, my father was just admitted to the hospital for emergency cardiac bypass surgery, having experienced a heart attack the day before. My father was young; only sixty-six years old and very healthy. Naturally, I was surprised and concerned, and I needed to get home! It was at the end of July, peak travel season in Europe, and I needed to get home, hoping that I would be able to see him again. Arriving at the airport, I was skeptical I would get a seat. I was blessed with a seat on a flight later that same day—a middle seat. That middle seat was the best seat on the plane.

Two years later, I was mistakenly assigned a middle seat on a flight from Frankfurt, Germany, to San Francisco, California—a twelve-hour flight. I am not talking about a middle seat in business or first class. I am talking about a seat in the middle of the middle section in economy. I was about to lose peace over it—no one would want the middle seat of the middle section on a twelve-hour flight! Especially someone who travels as much as I do. Unless, I thought to myself, it was the last seat on a flight that I desperately needed. I wasn't going to be able to change my seat; I needed to simply change my mind to come back into peace and experience happiness on the flight. As I prepared to board the plane, I visualized myself being happy in a middle seat. I saw myself smiling, feeling content, and being grateful to just have a seat on a plane going home like I was when my father was in the hospital. I said a prayer expressing to God my willingness to think of the experience differently and asked him to heal my mind. Again, a miracle! It was a pleasant flight. I was content and well rested when I arrived in San Francisco. The circumstances did not change; the only thing that changed was my mind. God has the power to change your mind. But he only exercises that power if you give him permission. He wants you to approach life with peace; he wants you to be happy and is willing to assist you. All you need to do is be willing to consider things differently, to think of things differently, and ask God to change your mind. It takes work; it takes constant vigilance to understand what you are thinking and be willing to ask God for help, but as you do, you will find there is a miracle waiting for you.

Perspective is a powerful thing. In criminal cases, attorneys on both sides know that eye witnesses are unreliable. This has been proven over and over again as multiple eyewitnesses who see the same events will give completely different versions of the "truth." We are all biased. We cannot escape being biased. I recently watched the 1957 movie *12 Angry Men* with Peter Fonda. This old black-and-white film is all about twelve men on a jury who sat on the same trial and needed decide the fate of the accused. Not one person on that jury heard the same thing, even though they listened to the same words. They each had a different perspective based on their biases.

We all see life and events through our own lenses, lenses that may be distorted and blurred by who we are, what we believe, what we are thinking, and how we feel. These biases cause us to judge unintentionally. Our perspective can have other consequences as well. There are times when our biases cause us to project our own intentions into a situation, clouding our vision to see it with love, kindness, and compassion.

Let me help you understand this better by sharing an experience from one of my clients. A few years ago, Cheryl and James were attending a high school choir concert where two of their teenage children were performing. James said that they weren't necessarily on a tight schedule, but he had an early start the next morning and was hoping to get home early. His wife, known as a social butterfly, loved to talk and visit with friends and acquaintances after the choir performances. That night, she lingered longer than usual, speaking to a friend or two. As their conversation turned to more personal subjects, James excused himself to go sit on the grass near the entrance. Several minutes later, Cheryl came out of the auditorium, and the first thing she said was, "It isn't fair that you get angry when I visit with my friends." But James was not angry; he was not mad. In fact, he was enjoying sitting on the grass, feeling the cool night air, relaxing, and feeling quite peaceful. It was Cheryl who *thought* he was angry, and those thoughts caused her to lose peace, creating a bias that was projected onto James. When James expressed that he was not angry, Cheryl didn't believe him because he had been angry in the past, and so surely he had to be angry this time. She came to the situation with her bias that James would be angry, and her emotions spawned around that perspective. She saw what she thought was the truth, but it was only *her* truth, not *the* truth. We can change our perspective by being willing to accept or consider that we may not be right. We are seldom right; we are almost always biased, and our perspective can cause us pain.

Henry Wadsworth Longfellow once said, "If you could spend one minute in the mind of your enemy, he would no longer be your enemy." It is true. When I was in law school, I did my best work when I could defend my opponent's case better than he could. When we can open our minds to accept that our bias and judgment is probably wrong, we can then be curious about what God's perspective would be and use that perspective as a basis for becoming happy. Recently I was in line at the airport and the person behind me was quite anxious for the line to move swiftly. He kept bumping into me with his bags and was speaking loudly and complaining. I turned around and offered him my place in line. He had as much right to get a ticket as I did, and there were probably circumstances he was experiencing that caused him to be anxious and upset. Rather than letting my thoughts turn negative toward him and be irritated myself, I turned the situation into one of service and compassion. He calmed down and was quite grateful. You can practice this kind of perspective every day. For instance, let the aggressive driver behind you move in front of you. Withhold a negative comment, smile and just relax. When your desire to become happy is stronger than your need to be right, or the need to be first in line, you will be well on your way to being happy. You can be at peace; you can live happily regardless of your circumstances.

Practicing positive perception

Let me recap this chapter with a few ways you can start to change your mind to have positive perception:

- Think of the person you have the most trouble with. It is not about them, it's about you. This person has positive traits; pick one and concentrate on that one thing. Do not consider anything else about that person. Do this for several days and the trouble you have with them will disappear.

- Think of a time or situation that has caused you pain or brings you unhappiness. Your mind is wounded. Now ask God to heal your mind, to change your mind. You may need to ask several times and truly be willing to have your mind changed, and the situation will become more positive. You will experience peace.

Points to remember

- You are in control. No one can change enough for you to be happy. It is all about you!

- You are not your ego. You are a creation of God. You have a divine nature.

- As you change your perception, your circumstances change, and negativity will disappear.

- Negativity is the result of a wounded mind. Ask God to heal your mind and restore you to peace.

- Your thoughts about others change your encounters with them.

- The ego will resist your desire to be happy. Persevere!

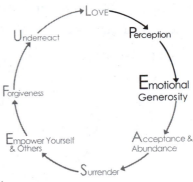

Chapter 3
Emotional generosity

You know you have emotional generosity when your primary goal is to bless the lives of those you encounter and interact with.

I am not a handyman. Not necessarily because I don't have the skills, but mostly because I don't have the right tools. When I have the right tools I can be a great handyman, but I have never taken the time nor had the money to invest in the right tools. Having the right tools is critical to any job or project. It is true with being happy as well. The next several sections are about the right tools. Not the only tools, but a few tools I have learned and developed to bring peace and be happy. So much of what we do and how we react to what happens to us is based on some internal script; this script is our tool box. The box of tools we use to fix things, people, and problems. These are the tools we have been taught to use as we experience life. For example, Jennifer is devastated whenever she is not acknowledged in a positive way. She grew up with very positive parents that complimented her and praised her excessively. If she is not praised, she does not feel valued or loved. As wife and mother of four, she battles depression and self-criticism because her husband and children do not value her by praising or complimenting her. She is living by an internal script; her tool box does not include the ability to find value without praise.

Our internal scripts are the tools we have been taught to use. Just as they have been learned, they can be unlearned. Unless we take the time to learn new tools, new ways of looking at things and of approaching daily life, we'll only get more of what we have experienced so far. You may desire to live a more satisfied life and desire to bring peace into your life, but may not know how or have the right tools. This book is designed to guide you through some simple yet significant principles and exercises that help you discover and develop new tools. These will bring you peace, satisfaction, and empower you to be happy.

Become less—be more

The concept of "self" is probably not new to you. You know of "self"-esteem, "self"-image, and so forth. I am sure you have encountered people you would label "self"-centered or "self"-ish. The whole idea of "self" is a combination of characteristics and traits that make up who you are. Your "self" has been formed through years of experience and training from parents, siblings, teachers, and employers. We are not the same person as when we were born, and we are not the same person we were last year or last week. Slowly, day after day, week after week, we become the person we are today. Some of our "becoming" has been deliberate, as we have read a book like this or taken a class or survived some crisis; other parts of our "self" were created unconsciously as events and situations occurred that shaped us into who we are. Our "self" is based on some inner yardstick, some magic formula that defines our success and importance. How you define your "self" is critical to your ability to be happy. The ego wants you to define your "self" based on the judgment of others, on material things such as your title, your job, your car, your body, your ideas and opinions, and even your political party. There is tremendous pressure to define yourself on things you have no control over.

I'm currently working on a Happiness Factor geared toward parents. In this manuscript, I challenge the common question, "What do you want to be when you grow up?" changing it to, "*Who* do you want to be when you grow up?" There is so much focus on being *something* that even as parents we concern ourselves with making sure our children "make something of themselves." We stress over what college they go to, what profession they choose, and how much money they will make. I am not saying these things are wrong, but the emphasis is misdirected. My suggestion is to concentrate on *who* our children become, not *what* they become. In reality, success has more to do with *who* you are than *what* you are. In my career, I have seen many people devastated by the prospect of losing their job. They had become so identified with their job that to lose it meant losing their self-identity. *What* they had become was more important than *who* they had become. When we give in to the ego and allow it to define who we are based on something other than our divine nature, we limit the peace and happiness we can experience.

Divine nature defines us all as equals. The ego causes us to misdefine our "self" as either superior to others or inferior to others, and these definitions lead to anxiety, offense, negativity, conflict, and unhappiness. The ego is fine with this because it uses these results to justify your own self-definition. This misdefinition of superiority or inferiority creates the misconception of self-importance. In a study of 537 dating men and women as reported in the July 22, 1986, edition of the *New York Times* by writer Daniel Goleman, who later authored the book *Emotional Intelligence*, "the researchers found that people who perceived their partners to be superior to them felt guilty and insecure. People who perceived their partners to be inferior to them reported feelings of anger. When partners perceived themselves to be equals, their relationships were relatively conflict-free and stable."[15] This perception is true in all our encounters and relationships. If we define ourselves as superior to others, we will find ourselves in conflict and will be constantly offended. If we define ourselves as inferior, we will constantly be looking for ways to impress others and gain approval. Our own definition of superiority or inferiority is sensed by anyone we encounter, and they will react to it.

It is this misdefinition that I call the "myth of self-importance." It is a myth because when we think of ourselves as important—more important than others—instead of bringing us peace and confidence, it brings the opposite. The more important you think you are, the less important others will consider you, and the more often you will be offended by those around you. If you find yourself in conflict with others and being offended, it is most likely your own misdefinition of self-importance that is causing it than anything else. Don't get me wrong. I think we are all important; we are all special and unique. The problem exists when the ego demands to prove your importance at the expense of others. Self-importance is a myth, it is a lie. We are all important, and no one is more important than another. When you take that attitude, you will find peace flow into your life. I challenge you to give up the self-definition created by the ego and consider that you are equal in importance to everyone. This allows you to become what I call "self"-less, and the miracle is that as you *give up* this self-definition, you make room for peace and happiness. As long as your self-definition is created by the ego and based on "what" instead of "who," there will not be room for peace. Make room; become more than you were before.

Emotional generosity

What does it mean to be "self"-less? It means giving of your "self"; it means letting your new self-definition based on your divine nature be shared with others. It means turning your heart and mind to compassionate thoughts and actions that benefit another person or persons. It has been called emotional generosity by Reverend Scott W. Alexander in one of his sermons. He says, "Emotional generosity is the quality of being *kind* and *welcoming* and *understanding* of persons around you…in all of their limitations, imperfections and flaws. Emotional generosity means that you give other human beings the benefit of the doubt, that you cut them some slack, and that you are slow to be harsh, condemning or judgmental."[16] This is the true definition of giving of yourself. Our self-definition created by the ego holds on to doubt in others. It hangs on to judgments and biases based on our own definition of how important we are. When we give this up, that act of *giving* is the ultimate in generosity; it is giving of your "self," and it is becoming "selfless." When you choose to be selfless, to give something of yourself to others, you will find greater peace and satisfaction. You will have more energy, and you will attract more generosity toward yourself. You know you have emotional generosity when your primary goal is to bless the lives of those you encounter and interact with. Here are some ways that I have learned to practice emotional generosity that I am sure will help you both understand and implement this in your life and be happy.

Turn your inward focus outward

Several years ago, my wife and I attended the Idaho State High School Basketball Championships. It was a well-anticipated battle between rival high schools for the state title. The game was close with both sides doing their best to the very end and with the wining shot hitting just at the buzzer. Our team won! Everyone was excited and happy, or so I thought. As I watched the team pass by us into the locker room, I overheard one player on the winning team complaining that his teammate was a "glory hog." At first I wasn't sure I heard correctly, but noticing the look on his face, I knew immediately that I had heard what he said. Though his team had won the state championship he was disappointed, angry actually, because he felt that his teammate "stole" the show and was a "glory hog." This should have been one of the happiest moments in his life, and yet he was unhappy. Without changing the circumstances, this young man could have relished in the win and could have felt satisfied and content. But he wasn't. Why? Because his emotion, attention, and desires were focused inwardly to satisfy the ego. We become more satisfied with life the more we share our "self" with others. In other words, the more we give our "self" away, the more we get in the way of peace and happiness. We gain by giving; we increase our satisfaction by serving others. Studies have shown that people who are "anxiously" engaged in serving those around them live a more satisfied life.[17]

It comes down to this: if you want to be happy, you need to turn your inward focus outward. This does not mean you give with resentment, that you do for others things that they should do themselves; it is more about "how" you do it than what you do. I have met and talked to a lot of volunteers that despise what they are doing but do it out of obligation. While giving and serving is good, if your heart and mind are not doing it with kindness and compassion it "*profiteth* you nothing." (1 Cor. 13:3) It is more about your motivations and attitude than what you do. It is about giving of your "self." It is about turning your inward focus outward.

Stop trying to impress

When you realize that we are all important and that in reality we are all equal, then there is no need to impress anyone. The need to impress arises when you feel inferior to someone or when the ego wants to be noticed. Be real; don't try to be someone you are not. This doesn't mean that you don't try to be a better person; of course you try to be the best person you can be. Often our attempts to impress someone will cause us to lie or exaggerate the truth or to put someone down to build ourselves up. When I finally learned this lesson, it brought peace to me. I realized that I felt stress and anxiety in relationships because I was constantly trying to impress the other person. Coming to understand myself and to know who I am—that I am a child of God and that I am loved by him even with all my limitations and inadequacies—reduced my need to impress. In other words, I allowed my definition of "self" to flow from my divine nature instead of from the ego. Now I find I can be more real, and being real means approaching every situation and every person with integrity and honor. By doing this, you give up the part of yourself that needs to be validated, and this brings peace to your life. When you no longer need to feed the demands of the ego, when you find true definition in your divine nature instead of your body, title, job, and other physical things, you are free to be who you are, and that freedom brings confidence, peace, and happiness. That alone is impressive enough without having to impress anyone.

Let others speak

Have you ever noticed how often people interrupt? Or how often you are interrupted? If you step back to observe and listen to conversations, you will be surprised at how often one person interrupts. Or, even better, how often one person will finish the other person's sentences as if to hurry them along to some conclusion or to just add their own two cents. I am sure you have had conversations with someone who can't wait for you to finish so they can talk. They are so busy thinking of what they want to say that they don't listen to what is being said. Having emotional generosity includes giving up on the part of your "self" that wants to interrupt or finish someone else's sentences. Be emotionally generous by listening to what someone else has to say—let them finish, let them have their say. You will be surprised at how much better you listen and how much better you feel. This also goes back to self-importance. When I observe people interacting, I can usually spot the person who feels superior and the person who either allows himself to feel inferior or is just insecure. If you are the one doing the interrupting or finishing sentences of the other person, then you are exerting superiority over them, and I can guarantee you that you are not getting 100 percent of the story. The other person will react to your exertion of superiority and will subconsciously or even consciously change the story because of it. There will be negative feelings in the interaction that reduce the amount of peace you can feel. Step back; let the other person have their say. Another element of emotional generosity is to share your spirit with them, to physically exert a loving spirit into the conversation, demonstrating that your intent is to hear them, to listen to them, to hear the truth. By outwardly focusing my spirit toward another, there is a greater openness in the interaction, and I find that there is faster rapport and honesty and that I learn more than I would have. The same is true if you feel insecure or inferior. Thoughts of inferiority will distract your listening, and you will fill in the blanks with information from your inferior position. I know you will be surprised at the peace and happiness you feel when you give others their say.

Perform service

A wise man once said, "When you are in the service of your fellow beings you are only in the service of your God." That is similar to the statement by Jesus when he said, "Inasmuch as ye have done it unto one of the least of these my brethren, ye have done it unto me." (Matt. 25:40) As we give of our "self" in service to others there is a positive energy that flows, and it is as if we are serving God himself. When we serve God, we are blessed with peace and contentment. However, there is another condition that we must consider. This is found in I Corinthians chapter 13, verse 3 where Paul says, "And though I bestow all my goods to feed the poor, and though I give my body to be burned, and have not charity, it profiteth me nothing." Paul, in his letter to the people of Corinth, gives wise counsel. He is saying that even when we give money or goods to the poor and do it without charity, it will not result in the positive results we desire. Surely it will help the poor, but for us it is as if we have done nothing. Why? Because you are not your goods, you are not your money, you are not material things, so when you give those things, though nice and valuable, it is not giving of your self. When those material gifts are given with an attitude of kindness, compassion, and love, peace flows into your life and you will be happy. Giving a gift begrudgingly or with resentment actually creates more negativity and conflict than if you had not given the gift at all. Serving others out of duty or resentment will be a negative experience and the ego will find all the justification needed to support why you were so burdened and bothered.

I challenge you to be generous with your self, give service, and find someone to serve each day. If you wake each day and ask God to show you someone who needs a helping hand, it will be done. I have practiced this, and I am surprised at what I have found that I did not see before. Not long ago, I was in the drive-thru at Taco Bell. I was coming home late from work and missed dinner, so I stopped to grab a bite to eat. I don't know why, but the car behind me caught my attention. I saw a mother and a young girl looking over the menu deciding what to buy. I couldn't hear them, and I had no idea what they ordered, but in my heart and mind I felt they were in need. When I picked up my food from the window, I asked to pay for the young mother's order. The person at the window told me they had only ordered one taco—for a total of $1.05. Two things passed through my mind. One, I was so surprised at the inspiration I had received and two, what a great opportunity to help a young mother in need and do it anonymously. Still at the window, I offered all my change, approximately seven dollars, to the car behind me to order whatever they wanted, and then I drove away. If the young mother accepted the offer or was grateful I will never know. This wasn't about money—seven dollars is hardly a generous donation. However, if I had to pay for the feelings of happiness I was feeling, it would have been worth much more than seven dollars! My experience of asking God to make me aware of those around me each day that need help has brought so much happiness to me. I have forgotten about my own worries, I have had a clearer mind, and I have found that I look at people differently now than I did before. Instead of judging them by their appearance, I am considering if they need help. I am feeling emotional generosity.

A small prayer each day asking for God to show me people whom I can serve has helped me approach each encounter with a compassionate heart instead of a selfish heart. I have turned my inward focus outward.

Express appreciation

Another form of giving of your "self" is to express appreciation and gratitude and giving compliments. I will cover gratitude in more detail in a later section, but let me just say that there is a very interesting sharing of feelings when you express appreciation and gratitude. We all like to hear the words *thank you*. They have an almost healing effect on us. Think of it, have you ever done something for someone that went unnoticed? Or worse yet, it was noticed but not acknowledged? It wounds us, and we need to be healed. The healing comes from expressing appreciation to everyone you encounter. This does not have to take the form of a "formal" thank you or be over exaggerated. Appreciation is shown in how you interact with the cashier at the grocery store, the server at the restaurant, or the person cleaning the bathroom. Judy tells this story. She was shopping at Macy's in the mall and went to the lady's room. The bathroom smelled fresh and was clean. When she exited the bathroom, Judy practically ran into the person who had just cleaned the bathrooms. She took a minute to say, "Thank you. The restroom was clean and smelled fresh. Thank you for doing a good job." The cleaning person started to cry and said that she had been there four years and not one person said thank you. It was overwhelming to her that someone would notice and then acknowledge it by saying thank you.

The flip side of expressing appreciation is learning how to take a compliment. How you take a compliment can either expand the generosity or minimize and destroy it. Your acceptance of a compliment is directly related to how you feel about yourself. So often I witness people minimizing or dismissing a sincere compliment when it is given. Are we afraid of success? Do we think that we don't deserve recognition? Many of us are afraid of appearing arrogant, and so when we are given a compliment or shown some appreciation, we dismiss it as if to appear humble. However, what happens most often is it diminishes the intent of the person giving the compliment. Because of my speaking and consulting engagements, I am often told how well I do. At first I would dismiss the compliment with some quip or comment that spoiled the intent of the person. I have since learned that the most appropriate response to any compliment or any expression of appreciation is to simply say, "Thank you," or "Thank you, I appreciate you saying that."

When you give, you get. In our youth, we all heard that it is better to give than to receive and it is true. The paradox is that as you give of your "self" you will find there is more of your "self" to give. The ego despises this thinking; the ego wants you to think that as you practice emotional generosity you are giving away something that can never be recovered. Don't listen to that lie. The ego wants you to believe you are more important than others and superior to them so that you don't need to give, you don't need to compliment or to say thank you or serve others. When you truly begin to realize that we are all equal, then you are empowered to act for yourself because you realize that there is no one more important than you. How often do we hold back giving of our "self" because we are hampered by thoughts of superiority or inferiority. When you strip those feelings away to where we are all equal in importance, you no longer feel the need to impress; you can serve without concern or resentment. Being equal in importance is a powerful and liberating fact. As you become less focused on your "self" and more focused on others, you will find that your "self" becomes more confident, able to handle anxiety better, and able to look at the world and the events around you with more clarity. This new and more confident "self" enables you to express appreciation to people around you and those you encounter each day. Your expressed appreciation reflects more of how you feel inside than what you feel outside. It is a better reflection of your divine nature. Aligning with your divine nature enables you to be happy.

Practicing emotional generosity

Emotional generosity is a mindset in itself, encompassing more concepts than space permits in this book. Let me recap this section with ways you can start to be emotionally generous and open your heart and mind to the great peace and happiness that will come:

- Think of someone you hold in high regard and highly respect. Now consider that you are their equal. Sure, you may not have done all they have done, but you are their equal. You are equally important. As you go about your day, consider that the people around you are your equal. They have as much right to be driving as you do; they have as much right to be in line at the bank as you do. When we are all equal, we no longer feel superior or inferior.

- I am sure you know someone who could use a boost right this minute. Stop reading and pick up the phone, get on e-mail, or walk over to their cubicle and pay someone a compliment.

- In your next conversation, don't talk. Just listen. Listen until it becomes uncomfortable, and then only say enough to keep the other person talking. You will be surprised how much you learn and how much better you feel.

- Ask God to show you someone who needs your help today—and serve them.

Points to remember

- You are equal in importance to everyone, so there is no need to impress.

- Take the time to listen, let others speak before you speak.

- Find a good cause to become anxiously engaged in, and look for people to serve each day.

- Each day find someone to compliment and appreciate, and accept compliments yourself with graciousness.

- Turn your inward focus outward through emotional generosity.

Chapter 4
Acceptance and Abundance

Living in real time is an acceptance of what is…and releases you from the ball-and-chain of the past, it frees you from worry about the future you cannot predict and enables you to live happily right now in real time…An abundance mentality happens when you direct your thoughts in a positive way, aligning your subconscious thinking with your conscious thinking to bring about a life without limits.

You are where you are. There is no way around it. However, I meet and talk to a lot of people who are not where they think they are because their thoughts are somewhere else. Cathy wants to be married and start a family. All she can think about is finding a husband and having children. She even has the names of her three future children picked out. She is so focused on the future prospect of being married that she did not notice the handsome man trying to get her attention in the company cafeteria. Cathy was not present, her mind was elsewhere.

You are where you think you are. Barbara is nostalgic and wishes for the good ol' days. She loved it when her children were young and wanted to be around her no matter what. She longs for the romance she shared with her husband when they first met. She misses the mountains where her family vacationed when she was a child. Barbara lives mostly in the past, missing great opportunities for peace and happiness in the present.

Where do *you* think about all day long? Do you find yourself reminiscing about the past or worrying about the future? Neither the past nor the future is real—they only exist in your mind. If you want to live happily—if you want peace—you need to learn to live in real time. There is no happiness in the past—only the memory of happiness. There is no happiness in the future—only the anticipation of happiness. Hindu Prince Gautama Siddhartha, the founder of Buddhism, is quoted to have said, "The secret of health for both mind and body is not to mourn for the past, nor to worry about the future, but to live the present moment wisely and earnestly."[18] If you desire to live happily—if you want peace—you need to find it here and now because it cannot be found in the past or in the future. The only time that is real is right now. You have no power in the past, nor do you have power in the future. Power to be happy is now, in this very moment. Don't let it pass. Right now is real time. *Now* is the time to be happy. Let me share a few examples of what I mean by real time.

Live in real time

On New Years day 1976, I was watching the Rose Bowl championship football game from fifty-yard-line seats. This was the biggest football game of the year, and I had some of the best seats in the stadium. It was partway through the game when my girlfriend asked, "Where are you?" She was perceptive enough to see that I wasn't really at the game—my head was somewhere else. I was worried about my scholarship, I was worried about my job, and I was worried about finals. Most people had paid a lot of money to see that game, and there I was, not even present enough to notice who was winning. I wasn't living in reality—I wasn't in real time. I was so worried about future events that I couldn't enjoy myself in the moment. It would have been better for me to not even be at the game. This shows that wherever our thoughts are is where we are.

For years Eric and Cynthia have been burdened with financial difficulties. Cynthia doesn't want to work; she would rather stay at home with the children. Though he has tried, Eric has been unable to find suitable work, requiring Cynthia to work full-time, and sometimes she has had to work two jobs. Cynthia bemoans the plight of having to work. Everyone around her feels her negativity as she complains. If she could accept the fact that she has to work, even though it is not her ideal situation, she could find peace. Living in real time includes accepting what is and then approaching it from a nonemotional stance.

I am sure you can relate to this example. I am constantly meeting new people, and it is embarrassing when I meet someone for the first time and just minutes later, I can't remember his or her name. Does that ever happen to you? I know that I don't have a problem remembering names, but I do know that if I am not present and paying attention when a person says his or her name I will forget it. It comes down to being present in real time when I meet someone.

Being present takes practice and patience. Part of my job requires me to be in many meetings and multiple teleconferences each day. I can't tell you how hard it is to stay present during those meetings. My mind wanders, and I find myself thinking about the past, dabbling with e-mail, or just doodling on paper. Invariably, I am asked a question or requested to comment on a certain subject and I had not been present enough to even hear the question. I then have to ask to have it repeated. It is embarrassing. Multitasking is not being present; it is a "rob Peter to pay Paul" scenario.

This last example is from when I was attending college and working on my undergraduate degree. Money was tight, and we could only afford one car. To help things, a close friend and I coordinated our schedules so we could carpool together. Over the many hours we spent together, I learned that my friend loathed renting and really wanted to own his own home. In fact, he would often say, "I can never be happy until I own my own home." I appreciated his goal and passion to own his own home, but many great moments were missed because he was so focused on the future that he could not appreciate the present. Owning a home does not bring you happiness. You can be happy whether you rent, lease, buy, or live with your parents. Happiness is not found in a future event; it is found right now, in this very moment.

If you are waiting for a new job before you can be happy, if you are waiting for Mr. or Mrs. Right to come into your life before you can be happy, if you are waiting for a wayward child to find his way before you can be happy, then you are missing the chance for peace and happiness in this very moment. I could have stood looking out the front window waiting for my mother to come back, but all the waiting in the world would not have brought her back. Don't get me wrong; I am not saying that you should abandon the past and pretend that it did not happen. It is a matter of learning from the past and making a conscious decision to live in real time. You should be mindful of the future, but not at the expense of the present. Our experiences, our adversity, our mistakes, as well as our triumphs, are valuable to the degree that we bring them to the present as a foundation for learning. I'm also not suggesting that you fail to plan for and look forward to the future—that is called hope. However, if you are caught up in the "what if?" syndrome of fretting over what could happen, then you are trying to predict the future, and that simply cannot be done.

I don't particularly like sports analogies, but I think this one is appropriate. If you are the quarterback of a football team and fumble on the first offensive play, how do you pick yourself up and move on to the next play? Do you worry about the next two or three plays, or do you focus all your attention on the current play? I think the answer is obvious; in order to be successful in football, you cannot be worrying about the last three plays nor can you be anxious about the next three plays—you must give your full attention to the current play. So it is with life; we are sometimes so consumed with thoughts of the past by reliving past mistakes that we are not even present in real time. Oftentimes we are consumed by "should have" thoughts, berating ourselves for poor decisions—things we should have done or could have done differently. These thoughts only lead to guilt, which leads to self criticism, which leads to negativity, which robs us of peace and happiness in the present. Another common problem is that we are so caught up with anticipatory anxiety about the future that we are not present in real time. If you are not present, you are missing real life. You are living in your mind because that is the only place where the past and the future exist. Just as it would be important to play football with a winning strategy that was planned ahead of time, we should also take enough care to learn from the past and strategize for the future. In fact, it is typically when we don't have a strategy that we are overcome with anticipatory anxiety. Paying too much attention to the past and worrying about the future transports you out of real time into an imaginary state that you cannot cope with. Start paying attention to where your mind is. Is it in the past, where you are reliving great moments, retelling great stories of adventure, stories of who did what to you, or great stories of conquests or mischief? The more time you pay attention to the past, either positive or negative, the more you are defining yourself as your past. But since the past only exists in your mind, you are creating an imaginary self-definition. Sure, we are all shaped by our pasts, but our experiences should be put into proper perspective to aid our present decision making and enhance our present quality of life. The goal is to be peaceful in real time, right now.

If you give life to the past, you energize the past, and it can rob you of the peace you could be feeling in real time.

Are you consumed by "what-if" thoughts, creating fear, worry, and anxiety over what is to come? You have no control over the future, and worrying about it will do no good. Don't disregard inspiration about something that needs your attention right now. However, it's important to remember that inspiration is different than those repetitive thoughts leading to anxiety. Those thoughts are based in fear—a fear that you are out of control, a fear of the unknown, and often your own feelings of insecurity. You cannot prevent what you cannot predict, and the future is unpredictable. Because now is the only time that is real, you need to think in present tense, bring that worry into the present, and decide what you can do about it. If there is nothing you can do, then surrender it to God and let him worry about it. Worry is a barrier to your happiness. When you are worried about the future through "what-if" thoughts, you are not present, and you are missing out.

If you are unable to find peace in your present situation, you need to do something about it. You can remove yourself from the situation, you can change the situation, or your can accept it for what it is. Eckhart Tolle, in his book *The Power of Now*, says there are no other options. He goes on to say, "If you want to take responsibility for your life, you mush choose one of those three options and you must choose now. Then accept the consequences. No excuses. No negativity. No psychic pollution. Keep you inner space clear."[19] Real time offers you these choices; the past offers no choices and neither does the future.

Accept what is

No one likes pain and so when the present is too painful we escape from real time to the past or future. I know about this. When I was going through chemotherapy, I found a corner of my mind where there was no pain, and I would escape to that place often because my real time was full of pain and thoughts of dying. My escape was a form of victimizing myself instead of accepting that I had cancer and that it was going to be painful. Partway through my treatment, I needed injections to stimulate my bone marrow to create white blood cells and prevent dangerous infections. The drug caused my bones to ache from the inside out, and every time a bone would move, I would experience sharp and burning pain. Even when I took a breath it caused my ribcage to expand and contract in a way that was extremely painful. After about four weeks, I told the nurse I didn't want the injection and told her to stop hurting me. With as much kindness as she could muster, she told me, "Kirk, it is going to hurt. It is supposed to hurt or you cannot grow the white blood cells your body needs. You are so tense that it is causing you more pain. You need to stop fighting it; you need to just accept that it hurts—that it is going to hurt." She was right. I was in denial; I was victimizing myself by complaining about the pain. Once I accepted that I was going to be in pain, I was able to deal with it by no longer fighting the pain and by being still enough to manage it better. More importantly, I didn't need to complain anymore because I had accepted the pain and taken steps to manage it. Our complaining only victimizes us. It is a form of denial that keeps us from addressing the issues in the present—in real time.

Acceptance is not agreement

Acceptance is not agreement. Acceptance is looking at something in totality without the need for judgment and without emotion. Neither does acceptance mean that something is right. For years I was unwilling to accept that I was an angry man. During a counseling session, my wife and I started to argue over whether or not I was an angry person. Our therapist finally said to me, "What harm would it do to accept that you are angry? Is that so bad?" He was right. Once I accepted that I was angry, I was able to identify my anger better and take care of it. Until then, I had been unwilling to look at my anger objectively and treat it.

You can accept something without agreeing with it. For several years my wife was telling me she had depression. I didn't understand it, and so I didn't accept it. By not accepting it, I was unable to really help her or learn more about it to help myself cope with her depression. I fought against it and wished that things could be back to normal. You see, I was wishing for the past, but the past no longer existed, so I was trying to live a fantasy. When I finally accepted her depression, I was able to support her recovery. The acceptance of her depression led us to peace. By denying her problem, I was preventing a solution—I was putting up barriers to finding peace. I have friends who have struggled with their son's homosexuality, and for years denied it, causing them to almost lose the relationship they had with their son. They were plagued with shame, intense feelings that they were bad parents, and guilt that they were bad people. Those emotions are unproductive and separated them from their son. Remember, acceptance is not agreement—and they didn't agree—but once they accepted that their son was homosexual, they were able to talk about it openly and learn that they could love their son even though they don't agree with his homosexuality. It is a matter of accepting what is, not wishing for what could be, that brings you peace.

Here is another example. After working for Hewlett Packard for seven years, I felt that I hated my job, and my manager was an easy target for everything that I disliked. I started blaming him and became the victim of his management style, his approach, and his personality. I was young at the time and didn't hold my tongue, and my complaining contaminated the entire team, turning them against our manager. As usually happens, there was a reorganization placing me in a different team reporting to a different manager. It wasn't long before I realized that it was not my previous manager that I disliked, it was the job itself. If I could have accepted I was dissatisfied with the job, I could have done something about it instead of losing peace over it and causing my coworkers to lose peace as well. Once I accepted that I didn't like my job, I started looking for another one. You see, I was in denial, and that denial made me the victim when all along I had the power to bring peace to my own life.

To further make this point, let me share the story of two dear friends, Joe and Sue. When there oldest son was nine years old, they noticed he had a hard time with simple things such as riding a bike and was not as agile as other boys his age. For years they noticed his coordination and posture deteriorate. Initial tests were inconclusive, and yet they knew something was definitely wrong. They continued their search for an answer while doing their best to treat their son's condition. When their son, Aaron, was fourteen, they discovered he had Friedreich's Ataxia (FRDA), which is a rare, genetic, life-shortening disorder affecting about one in fifty thousand people in the United States. The onset of symptoms is usually between the ages of five and fifteen. Aaron's prognosis was not good, and now Joe and Sue faced the daunting task of having to witness their son slowly deteriorate physically with a life expectancy of thirty to thirty-five. A few years later, Joe and Sue would learn that their youngest daughter, Allison, also had the disease. In Joe's own words he says, "For years I was angry—at the disease, at them, at God. My anger didn't help. During the years when I wasn't angry, I denied the disease existed, I avoided even looking at it—and that didn't help either." As the years have passed and their son's condition has deteriorated, both Joe and Sue have learned that acceptance is the most effective key to coping. Joe goes on to say, "I have discovered that this too can be a blessing in my life; it simply depends on how I choose to look at it...on my best days, I realize that this disease teaches me to 'stay in the moment.' Fear of the future and remorse over the past are of no useful value aside from how I might apply those hard-learned lessons in the here and now—I can choose to decide differently today. I am discovering that life is best when I stay in the moment, in the present."

In my talks with Joe and Sue, I have learned that their acceptance of this dreadful and incurable disease is the one thing that has benefited them the most. For years they were in denial, experiencing anger, frustration, and disbelief. Once accepted, they were able to turn their attention to positive things. Sue organized and created the first online parent support group for Friedreich's Ataxia which now provides information and support to 350 families facing the same disease. [20] Ultimately, this support group grew to become worldwide and fostered a research organization dedicated solely to FRDA and congressional awareness of the disease. Until there is acceptance, there is denial. As long as there is denial, there is no progress.

Aaron, now thirty, has as high a quality of life as he possibly can. He is active, lives in a wheelchair-accessible home designed by his father and built by the community. His mind is not affected by the disease, so he is bright, charming, and full of life even though his body is slowly failing. "This disease teaches me that we are not our bodies," Joe says. Being angry at the disease did not help. Blaming God, genetics, ancestry, or other factors did not help. Denying the disease and their son's condition did not help. Keeping it hidden and not telling anyone did not help. What helped was acceptance. Did they wish it did not happen? Sure they did. But like so many other things in life, wishing something did not happen keeps the very thing you despise from becoming one of the greatest blessings in your life. You can be happy regardless of your circumstances, even when they seem insurmountable and devastating.

Accepting what *is* enables you to live in real time. When I am angry, I am now able to accept that I am angry and take steps to relieve that anger, rather than denying it and causing it to fester. If I resent someone, I accept that too, and then I take steps toward forgiveness and peace. Acceptance is an enabler. It doesn't mean you agree with someone or agree with the circumstances or the situation; it means that you are willing to work on it. Denial is a barrier to peace. Try acceptance, and find the peace it can bring you. When you are unwilling to accept what *is*, you create inner conflict that creates negative energy. This creates a barrier to being happy. Acceptance of what is removes the unconscious conflict, opens your heart, and brings peace to any situation. If your present situation is painful, contentious, or negative, even devastating—if you find yourself complaining about what so-and-so did—it is time to accept what is and deal with it on a more peaceful level. It will bring healing and peace and empower you to be happy.

Be curious

So often we approach conversations and other interactions with the intention of delivering a message rather than learning or just listening. Even if our primary purpose is to understand something, we most often end up doing all the talking. Our internal intent sends an implied message to the other person. This message can be verbal or nonverbal, and it is what steers our agenda for the conversation. Being curious first and suspending judgment allows you to see people differently—to see them as they are. You see them in real time.

Being curious is a form of being present—it's a way to live in real time. Too often we have our own agenda in conversations—an agenda that prevents us from really listening and getting to the truth. This is very similar to the fifth habit in Stephen R. Covey's book, *The 7 Habits of Highly Effective People*.[21] In this habit, Covey counsels the reader to develop empathetic listening, which is listening with the intent to understand by getting inside the other person's frame of reference. One way to do this is to develop curiosity about the other person and what they have to say. This is not a technique as much as it is the principle of seeking first to understand before you are understood. Being curious means being present with the other person without baggage from the past or worry about the future entering into the conversation. The baggage from the past may appear in the form of resentment, dislike, or even things you have heard about the other person. No matter how hard you try to ignore the past, your mind will interpret everything in the context of your resentment, creating a mental argument of who is right. Being curious means giving deference to the person you are conversing with in order to hear his or her side of the story—to move from a messaging posture to a learning posture in the conversation. Have your children ever said, "You never listen to me"? Chances are you do listen to you children, probably more than they realize. However, what your child might be saying is, "You are not interested in who I am, and I need you to be curious about me." My children get a bit frustrated by me asking so many questions until I remind them that I am asking questions to make sure I am listening to what they have to say.

I am not suggesting that you will never have a message to deliver or that you shouldn't ever have an objective for a conversation; I am saying that you should approach each conversation from a position of learning. A position of learning allows you to stay present in the conversation instead of mentally tuning out the other person because you are so concerned about what you have to say. This is particularly true when you have a difficult message to deliver. When we have a difficult message to convey, we typically approach the conversation from a position of certainty—certain that we know the whole story, that we know all there is. When you shift to a more curious stance, a position of learning, the message is not as difficult to deliver. Being present means that you will abandon blame, stop arguing about who is right and who is wrong, and stop assuming that you already know the other person's intentions. Being curious demonstrates that you are in the game and that you are present; it demonstrates concern and can help you find a more suitable solution. In many cases, it will enable you to deliver the difficult message more effectively. If you can cultivate a curious approach in your conversations and your meetings, you will find that you are not only able to stay in real time, but you are also much more effective. You will find a greater rapport with others; you will find that others will volunteer to help you sponsor your agenda instead of their own. This has been a key success factor in the partnership conferences I have spoken at and with the alliance managers I have mentored. When you demonstrate real intent through curiosity, you demonstrate a real interest in the other person, and you stay in real time and bring peace to the situation.

I just don't get it!

Do you ever wonder why people do the things they do? Have you ever wondered why your husband can't put the lid back on the toothpaste or your teenager can't seem to get dishes into the sink when he is quite able to get them out of the cupboard and fill them with food? Why do people do the things they do? I just don't get it! No matter how often we ask this question—no matter how much we really want to know—the truth is, we may never know. Everybody has quirks, mannerisms, and habits that can really annoy us. Have you ever said, "I just don't understand why so and so does what he does?" For many years, my oldest son kept a strange schedule; he would stay up until three or four in the morning and sleep until two or three in the afternoon. For the life of me, I just could not understand that kind of a schedule. I just didn't get it! Maybe you have been hurt—terribly hurt by a friend—and as you rack your brain, you can't understand why it happened. Or perhaps your brother, who never smoked, is diagnosed with lung cancer, or your sister's fiancé was killed by a drunk driver. You watch the news and all you see is pain and suffering, and you wonder why it can all be so bad.

It isn't just at home, either. Maybe you apply and interview for a new job, knowing that you are the best candidate, and yet you don't get the job. Or your coworker, who is also a friend, steals the credit for the work you did together. There is so much in our lives that begs an explanation. And yet there is so much that just can't be explained. The more we try to understand it, the more anxious, worried, and afraid we get. Another aspect of living in real time is learning to let go of understanding. In Isaiah, God says, "Neither are your ways my ways."(Isaiah 55:8). There are things in this world that we just cannot understand, and as long as we hold out for understanding, we will not be able to accept or deal with the problem.

Whenever we ask why, we are trying to understand. I am not saying that you should never ask why; I am saying that there comes a point when you either give up on understanding and accept things for what they are and have peace, or you hang on to the need to understand and create a barrier to happiness. When I was diagnosed with cancer, I never asked "why me?" It just didn't matter, because as long as I was asking "why is this happening?" I was not trying to find a solution. As long as I asked "why," I was not working on "what" I could do to minimize the disease, to be healed, and to maintain a good quality of life. If your husband has asked you for a divorce, you may spend the rest of your life trying to understand why, and as long as you continue to ask, you will not be able to accept it and find peace. Again, acceptance does not mean that you agree; it means that you are taking the news seriously enough to deal with it by changing the situation, removing yourself from the situation, or accepting it for what it is.

The myth of multitasking

I have a friend who claims that multitasking is a lie, and I agree. We are constantly bombarded with multiple requests for our time. We have e-mail, instant messaging, the telephone, cell phones, and junk mail. Not to mention the TV and the Internet. All of this comes on top of the demands from our jobs, our immediate and extended family, our children, and our friends. Many of us try to cope with all of this through feeble attempts at multitasking. But multitasking is a myth. If you think that you are being effective at all of the things you are trying to do at the same time, you are living the lie of multitasking. In my various meetings, there are always people trying to listen to the meeting while using their Blackberry or checking e-mail. They are only partially present, and the effectiveness of the meeting is degraded because people who are supposed to be present aren't really there. Multitasking is a juggling act at best and a disaster at worse.

For many years, I worked in Los Angeles, California, with a ninety-minute commute each way. Though the commute was long, it was a great transition from work to home. In 1990, we moved to Boise, Idaho, and my commute was less than ten minutes each way. While this may sound great, the commute was too short to provide the nice transition from working to being at home. It was so short that it took me a long time to be present at home because my mind was still at work. Where is your mind when you are at home? If it is not at home—if it is still at work—if you are thinking about all that you didn't get done or all that you have to do tomorrow—then you are not in present in real time; you are putting your attention on the past or worrying about the future. Regardless, your family will feel that you are not present and start treating you like you are absent.

During the dark period of my life that I explained in the introduction, I started to feel quite lonely, and it wasn't because I wasn't around people, it was because I was absent from most situations. I just wasn't present, and it went on for so long that my children and my wife started treating me like I wasn't there. The truth is that I wasn't. I started blaming them; I started to have very dangerous thoughts of loneliness, of being alone when surrounded by people—a very acute form of loneliness. It took me awhile to realize that they were only reacting to my mental absence and not to me as a person. It took some work, but I was able to start being present. When I was at home, it took surrendering to God the things that I didn't get done that day and having faith that I would have the time and strength to get them done the next day.

When you multitask, something always gets lost. It is a win-lose or lose-lose proposition. If you don't believe me, just watch the look on your spouse's face when you take a business call in the middle of a conversation. You just robbed your spouse of your time in order to pay attention to someone else. If you don't believe me, keep using your e-mail while you pretend to talk to your son about his homework. It just doesn't work. It takes courage to say no to multitasking, but the benefits are enormous. Being present means you give each task the attention it deserves, and you end up being more productive than when you split your time between several tasks. Don't get me wrong, I am not saying that you should stop managing your time; I am proposing a time-slicing approach, where you juggle many balls by giving them the time they deserve rather than tying to do them all at the same time. Set some boundaries for yourself so that you don't become a slave to the multitask-master.

Redefine quality time to make it NOW time

As a young father, I would often hear people say, "Enjoy the moments you have with your children now because before you know it, they will be gone and married." They were right. Before I knew it, my children were grown and on their own. It doesn't mean that my job is over and that I can't have a healthy relationship with them; it means that lot of quality time slipped by. We only have "now" time, and whether it is "quality" time or not, we need to take advantage of it. I often work at home, and I make it a point to drop what I am doing in my office when my children call me. There have only been a few times when I wasn't able to do that. It's not that I am special or that I don't have a lot to do, I just decided that "now" time is more important than waiting for "quality" time.

About ten years ago, my aunt Beverly passed away after a long and difficult battle with breast cancer. She was one of the nicest and warmest people you would ever meet. She was young at the time, survived by her two children and her husband. Her funeral was more like a family reunion for me, as I became reacquainted with many of the extended family who I had not seen in years. My aunt passed away without knowing how much I admired her and looked up to her as an example of how to be happy despite adversity. I felt guilty and ashamed as I stood over her grave, realizing that the opportunity to tell her how I felt had passed. In that moment, I vowed to not let that happen again. I promised myself that I would express appreciation for those around me regularly and do it often enough that if anything were to happen to them, I would not feel as miserable as I felt at my aunt's funeral. Don't wait to express love and gratitude for others, because the opportunity may be gone tomorrow. Don't wait for the perfect moment, because it may not ever materialize. You need to redefine quality time into "now" time—into real time.

When my children were young, I also made it a point to never drive anywhere alone. If I had to run to the hardware or grocery store, I would invite whoever wanted to go with me. On the way, we would stop for a treat at 7-Eleven or some other convenience store. No one would say that driving in a car and doing errands was quality time, but it was "now" time. Today, my children recount fond memories of getting slurpees at 7-Eleven when all I was doing was trying to spend time with them, regardless of whether or not it was quality time. If I had waited for quality time to be with them, it would never have happened. Redefining quality time as "now" time brings you into the present instead of waiting on the future.

Like what you do

There are too many of us who seek to do only those things we like to do. I don't know of anyone who has that luxury—the luxury of not doing anything that he or she doesn't want to do. It's a fantasy. When I was in high school and college, I worked at a meat-packing plant. If you have ever seen the inside of a meat-packing plant, you might not ever eat meat again. I didn't like the job, but it paid the bills. I could wake up every morning and loath going to work seeing all the blood, guts, and mess, but I chose to like what I did instead of doing only the things that I liked. It is so easy to complain about the things we have to do. It is a much harder but more rewarding goal to like what we do—to find something about what we are doing right now to like. Albert E.N. Gray's essay "The Common Denominator of Success" is as poignant today as it was in 1940 when first delivered. He says, "The secret of success of every man who has ever been successful—lies in the fact that he formed the habit of doing things that failures don't like to do."[22] We often find ourselves in a situation that we cannot change immediately and have to persevere while we take steps to change it. This can be difficult. If you have a job you dislike, it may take you months to find a new job. During those months, you can either live in misery, or you can find peace by accepting that it will take time to find a new job and then surrender this to God by asking him to open your eyes to see what is positive about what you do. You can ask for the miracle of liking what you do. It enables you to stay in the present even though it may not be ideal.

Liking what you do means learning to savor the journey, to enjoy getting there as much as arriving. "Are we there yet?" is the age-old question from your children in the backseat of the car. They just can't wait to get to wherever they are going. It is annoying and hard to deal with when every two minutes the same question is asked. I don't know of any parent who doesn't find that frustrating. I have heard stories of parents getting so upset by the repeated question they have simply just turned around and gone back home. Yet, as adults, don't we ask the same question over and over again? Maybe not in the same words. But when we are impatient with God for not blessing us when we want something and we have to wait longer than we think we should, aren't we asking the same thing? Perhaps we are experiencing a trial in our lives, and we want nothing more than for it to be over. Just as we want our children to learn to enjoy the journey—to take pleasure in the process—we too should take that same attitude. In most cases, there is no amount of worry or concern that will change the outcome, so you might as well find peace along the way. Again, it is a matter of accepting what *is* instead of focusing on what *should be*.

My whole life I have struggled to find pleasure in the journey. I have most often kept my sights on the goal in mind. I prided myself on planning ahead, reducing surprises, and keeping my destination in mind. But there was so much I missed along the way. I missed things that could have brought me happiness and peace because I was looking elsewhere. Now, I am learning to find beauty in the smallest of things. I am learning to look for the beauty around me, to ask God to open my eyes to beauty. Whereas before I was critical and judgmental, I now see things that I never before noticed. There is beauty everywhere; you just have to see it. As an exercise, find the most innocuous thing you can think of and look at it until you find beauty. Don't just think about doing this, really *do* it. Find something that you think is average, simple, or even ugly. Look at it; study it. Move around and look at it from different angles—look at it in different light—and as you study it, you will start to notice things you didn't notice before—you will start to find beauty in things you haven't paid attention to. It is like the note on the refrigerator door—the note you put there to remind yourself of something important. You end up looking at it so often that you actually stop seeing it, and it becomes invisible. It is the same with so many things in our life. We become used to them, and we don't see the beauty of it any more. For this exercise, I choose to look at the cement curb by the sidewalk. I am sure you would agree that there is nothing special about a cement curb. For the most part I never think of cement curbing unless it is raining or I am parking. But for this exercise, I sat on my front lawn, and for several minutes, I studied the cement curb. I saw someone's handiwork, I saw lines, flaws, chips, and stains, and then I saw beauty where I did not see it before. If you want to, you can see the beauty and wonder in anything. Living in real time also means paying attention to the things around you and finding the beauty that abounds in your life.

For several months, I spent a lot of time in Heidelberg, Germany. Heidelberg is a beautiful city visited by thousands of tourists each year. When I first started visiting Heidelberg, I was in awe of how the church bells sounded when they rang. At certain times, several churches ring their bells at the same time, filling the town with music. The bells were so loud they woke me during the night. I have now been to Heidelberg enough that I barely even notice the church bells. What a shame that something so wonderful and so beautiful has lost its beauty. Or has it? The bells have not changed; I have. The bells sound just as charming as they once did, but I no longer hear them that way. Now when I visit, I make a point to stop and listen to the bells. It is a reminder to live in real time, to value the present, and to like what I am doing. We all feel better when we are surrounded by beauty, and it's important to remember that we are all surrounded by beauty every day. The beauty around you can lift you up and can bring you peace. Finding the beauty that abounds enables you to like what you do, to like where you are. It keeps you present instead of escaping to the past or the future.

Real time—real happiness

Living your life in real time brings real happiness. It gives you the power over any circumstance that causes you to lose peace or experience pain. By observing where your thoughts are during the day, you can bring them to the present. It is about turning your unconscious thoughts into conscious thoughts and directing them toward happiness rather then letting them contaminate your present moment with negativity. Recently, I was with my father at the hardware store. As we approached the checkout counter, the cashier asked how my father was doing. He said, "I can't complain. I've tried it, and it doesn't do any good." How right he is. Complaining doesn't do anyone any good at all. Any time you are complaining you are resisting what *is*, and that resistance creates conflict that is felt by everyone around you.

Indeed, there are times when you need to shed light on something that is dissatisfying, but it doesn't need to be done in the form of a complaint. Recently, my wife and I were out to dinner, and her salmon was not cooked correctly. I am sure it was just a mistake, and not something that required us to complain, but it was definitely something we needed to call attention to. How would you handle that situation? Would you be offended, or would you simply say that the fish is not cooked to your satisfaction? To accept what *is* means to focus on the fact that the salmon is not cooked, rather than focusing on how it happened or who is to blame. In this case, the server took the salmon back to have it prepared correctly. To our benefit, the manger came to our table informing us that our meal was free. There was no argument, no blame, and no lack of peace. This can be the same for you. Complaining doesn't do any good. When someone is complaining, I like to use the phrase, "The grass is greener where you water it." This is a twist on the old saying, "The grass is greener on the other side of the fence." When you feel the temptation to complain, start to interpret it as a clue that you need to take some action—that you need to "water the grass." You need to change the situation, remove yourself from it, or accept it.

Living in real time is an acceptance of what *is*. It is being curious about others and the situation. It is about abandoning blame, and it releases you from the ball-and-chain of the past; it frees you from worry about the future you cannot predict, and it enables you to live happily right now in real time.

Developing an abundance mentality

As far as I can tell, Stephen R. Covey was the first person to popularize the concept of an abundance mentality. In *The 7 Habits of Highly Effective People*, Covey introduces the concept as one of three character traits needed to develop habit four: think win/win. Covey explains that the three character traits needed for a win/win paradigm are *integrity*—the value we place on ourselves; *maturity*—the balance between courage and consideration; and *abundance mentality*—the paradigm that there is plenty out there for everybody.[23] Since Covey's use and explanation of the abundance mentality, it has become widely applied as both a principle and a technique to attract abundance into our lives, careers, and bank accounts. Some of today's writers teach about abundance mentality as a secret to acquire wealth and riches. While wealth and riches are certainly a very real by-product of an abundance mentality, they are secondary to the abundance of happiness and peace that are attracted into your life. Abundance is God's gift to the world and to you. An abundance mentality is the mindset that there are no limits to your potential, no limits to the good that can happen to you and on your behalf. It represents an abundance of all that is good and suggests that there is more than enough for everybody. Imagine yourself standing in line to buy tickets to a movie. The line is long, and you wonder if the movie will sell out before you have a chance to purchase your tickets. How do you react when a few yards in front of you a family of five jumps the line? You could get angry, upset, and lose peace over something as trivial as cutting in line. I am sure this has happened to most of us, and it's unpleasant. What if on the other hand, you knew that there were enough seats—good seats even—for everyone in line? Would your reaction to someone cutting in line be different? Certainly it would. You would be less anxious, more confident, more secure, and at peace. You might even invite someone to cut in front of you. An abundance mentality is just that: confidence and security that there is plenty for everyone, reducing the stress, fear, and anxiety over having to hurry to get your share.

As I approached my last year in college, I wanted nothing more than to work for Hewlett Packard. After several interviews, I was sure I had the job but later found out that a close friend of mine was offered and accepted the job I applied for. I faked congratulating him when inside I was seething with anger. I had to take another job, feeling like a complete loser. This was clearly a scarcity mindset, and it caused me to feel depressed, anxious, and angry at my friend and the world. All I could see was what I didn't have. I started to doubt myself and my abilities. Worst of all, I started to believe that great jobs weren't meant for me, and my self-confidence took a nosedive. I felt incapable of finding a good job and would have to settle for what I had.

Several weeks later, Hewlett Packard called me back to interview for another position, and within two days I was hired! All of my worrying and anger accounted for nothing! I could have done all I did to get the job without the negativity and anger. It was wasted emotion and energy. This year I will have completed twenty-four years at Hewlett Packard, and it has been a great career. Is this just a story about my own personal woes? Is this just a story with a happy ending? No, I tell this story to illustrate that I had to learn a hard lesson: that just because one door closes doesn't mean they all close. It's a well known cliché, right? Well, yes, but it is only a cliché because it is overused and misunderstood not because it isn't true. I have since learned that the only limits I put on my life are the ones I fabricate in my own mind. Success only has to be a struggle if we think it is. I should have been grateful for a job and been truly happy for my friend, rather than faking it. Instead I was miserable; I had wounded my self-confidence, and I lived with fear.

How many times do we publicly congratulate someone for an award or an accomplishment when inside we are really thinking that he or she doesn't deserve it and wish him or her bad luck or misfortune? How often have we heard of someone's misfortune, such as a car accident or losing a job, and say to ourselves, "It serves them right! They deserved it!" We criticize and put others down to lift ourselves up as if there is justice in it. This is a scarcity mentality. We interact with people who have a scarcity mentality every day. You recognize them as the driver who won't let anyone into traffic, the person who is unable to give credit, and those who are constantly critical of others. People with a scarcity mentality can also be recognized by their continual victimization, their blaming others for their own mistakes and misfortunes, and their obsessing over possessions. Complaining, competitiveness, and accusations of disloyalty are all signs of a scarcity mentality. A scarcity mentality is a mindset of limits and boundaries when none really exist. Placing an imaginary limit on the good in the world and the good that can happen to us is a scarcity mindset. The more we give in to this scarcity thinking, the more it becomes our way of life.

Where does this scarcity mentality come from? We certainly weren't born with it; in fact, it is the opposite. We come into this world with an abundance mentality, thinking that anything is possible. In our youth and innocence we think we can be anything we want to be—that we can do amazing things. Through the teaching of others and even our own mistakes, we learn to limit ourselves. Where we once saw possibilities and potential, we now see hardship, pain, boundaries and impossibilities. We pursue *what to be* rather becoming *who we should be*. Unfortunately, that is an outside-in approach rather than an inside-out approach. In elementary school when we were taught to color within the lines, we took it literally and applied it to our whole lives. It is so "natural" to feel bad when something good happens to someone else that we really realize we do it anymore. The ego creates boundaries and limits, and when you ignore the abundance of life, you are giving in to the ego.

Let's take a look at an example of this. When Lisa walks into her house, she notices everything that's wrong with it. It is too small, it is not clean, the furniture is old and outdated, the carpet is the wrong color, and the appliances are not new. All her friends have nicer houses, and the more she visits them, the more she hates her own house. Lisa is stuck in a scarcity mindset, only noticing what she does not have instead of the great blessings she could experience by truly feeling happy for her friends. Just because her friends have nice houses does not mean that she does not or that she can't. An abundance mentality exists when we are able to feel happy for others as if they were ourselves.

An abundance mentality is a new way of thinking that involves several of the other transforming concepts presented in this book, starting with our divine nature. Our divine nature is limitless and full of love, peace, and compassion. Our divine nature exists in abundance where there is no limit to the good and the happiness available to us. An abundance mentality occurs when you align your thinking with God and understand that miracles do and will happen for your benefit. An abundance mentality happens when you direct your thoughts in a positive way, aligning your subconscious thinking with your conscious thinking to bring about a life without limits. Abundance is more than just positive thinking. It is a mindset that leads to compassionate and loving behavior while bringing you rewards and peace. An abundance mentality is something that you can learn. Later in this chapter I explain four steps to put an abundance mentality in to action.

The law of attraction and the law of the harvest

The very foundation of an abundance mentality arises from our way of thinking. When you say to yourself, "I hate being overweight," you are attracting into your life what you really don't want, and you are thinking with scarcity. If you say, "I hate being poor," that too is a scarcity mentality that will actually attract poverty into your life. You will be "poor" regardless of how much money you make because that is your mindset. If you complain about your partner or spouse focusing on all he or she does that is irritating and annoying, you will actually find more about he or she that you don't like. Your thoughts have a direct and real impact on your body and your health. If you are overweight, then you have probably tried and failed at one diet after another. You are tired of being overweight, and you may just accept the fact that this is who you are. You can change your circumstance by changing how you think. By saying "you hate being overweight," you are directing your mind to "being overweight," and you will attract that into your life. Each thought is like a seed you plant. You can't plant lemon seeds and expect to grow peaches. A lemon seed can only grow lemons.

If you want peaches, you must plant a peach seed. The same is true with your thoughts and your intentions. Your negative thoughts and negative intentions will grow and attract negativity into your life. Positive thoughts and positive intent reap positive and constructive results. There is no other way; it is a law of nature. We attract into our lives what we think about. If you have depressive thoughts, you will have depression; if you have unhealthy thoughts, you will be unhealthy. These are all signs of a scarcity mentality. You can transform your scarcity mentality to an abundance mentality by changing your mindset. Abundant thoughts, or thoughts stemming from an abundant mentality, produce a positive outcome. If you think of yourself as healthy, you will attract more energy and strength into your life. If you think of yourself as being thinner, you will find it easier to lose weight. Your mindset is magnetic, and it contains an intense power of attraction. An abundance mentality is more than positive thinking; it is the act of positive intentions. It starts with a desire to live an abundant life with the intent to cast out doubt and insecurity and live more by faith. It means believing that there is more than enough to go around; more than enough love, compassion, wealth, success, admiration, and even respect. Let's explore a few concepts to help you develop an abundance mentality.

Have a gratitude attitude

When our children were young, we had a set of sing-along tapes that we played all the time. One was called *Gratitude Attitude* with a catchy tune and words that were easy to remember. It soon became a catchphrase in our family. Instead of having to tell our children to say "thank you," we simply had to say, "Have a gratitude attitude." It always surprises me how few adults have a gratitude attitude and instead have an attitude of entitlement; a mindset that the world owes them something. With that mindset, they become myopic to the world around them and can only see what they lack instead of the marvelous and great blessings they enjoy each day. If you find you are lacking, then you are finding exactly what you are looking for. It is not conscious seeking that causes you to find the lack in your life, it is subconscious, and you have created a habit of not even noticing things around you for which you can and should be grateful.

Developing an abundance mentality requires training yourself to see the abundance that is already in your life through gratitude. No matter what your circumstances are, you have something to be grateful for. As you are reading this book, be grateful for your ability to read. There are a lot of people in this world who cannot read or do not have proper eyewear to read. If you have eaten today, be grateful for food to eat. There are many people, probably people in your own town, who will go hungry today. The first step in acquiring an abundance mentality is to be grateful.

Here is something I recently learned at a conference where Colleen Covey Brown gave a class on writing a gratitude journal. Get a notebook and a pen and set them by your bedside. Each night before you go to bed, write down three things you are grateful for. Do this for three weeks, and you will have developed the habit of being grateful. I challenge you to do this. You will have a feeling of peace flowing into your mind and into your life. You will start to see your life differently. Additionally, you will start to see and feel grateful for things you haven't noticed before. Gratitude opens up your mind to see beauty, and it has the power to attract into your life more to be grateful for. Make it your daily purpose to find something to be grateful for, and you will be amazed at what you find. Gratitude is the very foundation of an abundance mentality and has enormous side benefits. Grateful people are healthier and happier. They have greater confidence in themselves and in their God. They are able to face adversity with dignity, and they have less fear. Being grateful attracts people to you and will provide you with richer and more intimate relationships.

Be generous

Discussion of an abundance mentality often centers on receiving abundance, but there is a giving aspect to it as well. We don't need to wait for our lives to be abundant in order to be generous. We can be generous even when our means are meager. Generosity is more than monetary donations; it includes all kinds of resources and is more about the act of generosity than what you give. Though it sounds like a Norman Rockwell painting, giving a plate of cookies to a new neighbor demonstrates tremendous generosity. In fact, sometimes it is the smallest of gestures that has the greatest impact on the people around us. A few weeks ago, my wife was driving through the neighborhood and waved to one of our neighbors out walking his dog. The following week at church he stopped my wife to thank her for waving. He had been having a bad day, and her smile and wave lifted his spirits and gave him hope. Generosity is an outward demonstration that you have an abundance mindset. You cannot expect to have abundance in your life if you hoard all that you have, including material goods and intangibles. Regardless of your situation and circumstances there is something you can be generous with. Let someone into your lane of traffic, hold the door open for someone, or help a neighbor. This summer we came home from vacation and noticed someone had washed our windows. Our neighbor saw the windows were dirty from a storm and washed them for us. This is generosity.

If you desire to live an abundant life, you also need to develop the desire to serve, to give, and to be generous. As you give, you will find that the law of attraction becomes active, and people will become generous with you as well. There is always enough to go around. Generosity is more about what you are feeling on the inside than how much you have in your pocket. It is a mindset. Consider this: if you are in a good mood today, do your best to give it away, to share it with those you encounter. Give a smile, a wave, a handshake, or a "thank you." These small acts of kindness are acts of generosity. Generosity is not just about giving *things*.

Often people wait to be wealthy before being generous, but often the opposite occurs. The more people get, the less generous they are. Possessions are possessive. They possess you; not the other way around. When you start to look at your house, your apartment, your car, and your clothes as gifts from God—as a demonstration of his abundance—you will start to lose your attachment to them, and you will begin to feel generous. They won't matter as much, and you will find that the ball-and-chain of your possessions has been removed and freedom has cropped up in its place. Be generous—be very generous—and you will find abundance flowing into your life. So often we believe that happiness is found in the accumulation of possessions. It could be your big house, your nice car, your pool. Yet there are so many people with fewer material possessions than you who are happy. Your possessions possess you—they cannot bring you happiness. Being generous with what you have opens you up to receiving more.

Stop comparing

True success and achievement is not about being better than someone else; it is about being better today than you were yesterday. Comparing ourselves to anyone else is self-defeating, as there will always be someone faster, smarter, better looking, wealthier, and healthier than you. This is difficult because the ego convinces you that you need to compare yourself to someone or something. Standing in line at the supermarket, you read headlines about the prettiest people in America, how to lose weight, how to have better sex, and how to look like a movie star. At work we are subjected to relative rankings and performance scales. Our children constantly face scrutiny and comparisons at school where they face grades on a curve, the homecoming court, and MVP awards. A few years back, we vacationed on a cruise ship, and my wife and I got a kick out of watching people check each other out doing mental calculations and comparisons of weight, age, and wealth as they walked by the pool. The ego demands to feel superior, so it is constantly pitting you against someone or something, feeding the myth of self-importance. The constant comparisons create a continuous stream of negativity in the form of competition between ourselves and the people around us. This especially happens between siblings and family members to the point where relationships are stretched to the limit and destroyed over competition and judgment. Comparing yourself to someone else is a veiled form of judgment. You are either judging them or judging yourself. Either way, it is unhealthy and unrealistic.

When I was young, my parents would often ask me, "Why can't you be like your brother?" It was the most ridiculous comparison because if they knew all the things about my brother that I knew, they would have never asked that. On the other hand, we often demand a comparison, thinking that we deserve something that someone else has. This creates a strong sense of inferiority, which, in turn, creates guilt and anger. Comparing yourself to anyone or anything else is a battle that cannot be won. An abundance mentality requires that you let go of comparisons and establish your own measure of success. Your value is in your creation and is based on your divine nature. You are and always will be who God intended you to be. You are a child of God, and that is the greatest of all of his creations. God's will and power are much greater than your own. Who does God think is more successful: the man who overcomes anger or the man who overcomes an addiction to alcohol? We could debate this question forever, but the truth is that there is no comparison! God is not going to compare us to someone else. That is only something that man does. Our goal is to improve, to grow, to become more like God, to overcome the ego, and to develop love, compassion, and joy. When you compare yourself to others, you limit yourself and you limit them. Comparing yourself to someone else or any thing else creates a scarcity mindset. This doesn't mean that we can't rely upon family and friends for emotional, moral, and physical support. To a large degree, those relationships determine our overall level of satisfaction. However, a study of more than eight thousand adults revealed that a person's level of happiness is reduced by 26 percent if he or she regularly compares the quality of his or her family and social relationships to that of others.[24] Comparing ourselves to others creates an unrealistic and unobtainable standard to live up to and leads to unhappiness. The mental act of comparing is a demonstration of a scarcity mindset.

There are at least three forms of comparisons that are dangerous: (1) when we compare ourselves to others; (2) when we have an unrealistic view of what success is; and (3) when we compare others to others, such as comparing your spouse, your partner, or your bother to someone else. All of these comparisons are a form of judging the value and worth of another—a judgment that should be left to God. When we place ourselves in an unrealistic position of success, we often feel guilty when we think about others' lack of success.

Let's imagine two brothers: Gary and Jeff, who are just one year apart. As they grew up, they attended the same high school, often had the same teachers, and participated in the same sports. Both got good grades and were hard workers. Jeff went on to a career in law, and Gary became a laborer and an alcoholic. Gary is proud of what Jeff has achieved as an attorney and has never held it against him. Jeff, on the other hand, has felt a tremendous amount of guilt because he is successful and Gary is not. For years he wallowed in guilt until he realized that it wasn't doing either of them any good. He realized that his guilt was actually a judgment of Gary and was an unhealthy comparison. Jeff's success in no way took anything away from Gary, and by feeling guilt, he was in a scarcity mindset, creating limits for himself and his brother. An abundance mindset is that there is enough success for both brothers. Jeff could have been at peace all these years instead of wallowing in guilt. Gary eventually recovered from alcoholism and has been sober for more than seven years. Who has had the greater success? Jeff, with his success in law, or Gary, who overcame alcoholism? The answer is neither because there is no comparison!

How quick we are to make comparisons when there is none to be made! Just the other day I overheard a discussion at church over who was more likely to go to heaven: someone who lives an unrighteous life only to repent just days before his death or someone who lives a good life only to fall away a few days before his death. The answer is that we don't know because there is no comparison. To have an abundance mentality is to acknowledge that you are your own measuring stick, and you are the only one who can determine if you are better today than you were yesterday. Remember, any time you are making a comparison, you have a scarcity mindset.

Replace "I can't" with "I haven't"

When does someone actually begin to play the piano? If you were to ask a beginning student if she plays the piano, most likely she would say, "No, I am just learning." Isn't learning to play the piano the same thing as playing the piano? I think it is. But we get so accustomed to saying the words "I can't" that we barely notice what we are really saying. How many times a day do you say the words "I can't" when in reality, the response should be something else altogether? If I ask my youngest son to take ash, most likely he will say, "I can't." Is that the truth? Surely he

—he is physically qualified and smart enough to take out the

trash. So why "can't" he? The fact is that he doesn't *want* to take out the trash. Society today lets us get away with saying "I can't" as the universal excuse for almost anything. Every time you say the words "I can't," you create a limit on yourself as a reflection of a scarcity mentality.

"I haven't," on the other hand, is an expression of an abundance mindset. If someone were to ask if I play the guitar, my answer is "I haven't yet learned." I am sure I can play the guitar if I choose to learn, and to say that I can't play the guitar is a limitation that just does not exist. I always joke that I can't sing. However, in truth, I can sing, I just choose not to sing as a courtesy to those who might be listening. The correct answer is, "I don't sing as well as I would like to."

There is a significant difference between saying "I can't" when you mean "I haven't." The words "I can't" limit your potential and send a strong message to your subconscious that if you were to try, you might fail. Failing is exactly the outcome of a scarcity mentality—you can't so you won't. Turning it around to be "I haven't" opens up the limitless possibilities of potential and creates a mindset of abundance without limits.

For several years, I have worked part-time in Germany. I am able to do business, eat, get to where I am going, and pay my bills without knowing how to speak German. I am often asked if I speak the language. It would be easy to say "I can't," but that phrase is too limiting. The truth is that I have taken several lessons and have tried to learn phrases in German, but "I haven't" invested the time to learn to speak German enough to converse. "I can't" means "I won't," but "I haven't" means that the potential exists for me to learn. You may think this is a silly word game, but our words reflect our mindsets, and when we have a mindset that limits our potential, we are operating from a scarcity mentality.

When you adopt a mindset of abundance, it becomes a new way of life, and you will find yourself shying away from anything that limits your potential. Let your words reflect your mindset of abundance.

Abundance mentality in action

I am constantly battling a scarcity mentality, shifting between scarcity and abundance on a daily basis. Though my goal is to practice abundance, it takes time and daily practice to become "centered" in abundance. When I have an abundance mindset, I am at peace with myself and the world. I am able to handle life's challenges with peace and calmness, and I am able to skillfully cope with daily adversity. An abundance mentality gives me the confidence to accept that there is no comparison and that I don't need to impress anyone. It solidifies the fact that I am equal to everyone else and abolishes the myth of self-importance. An abundance mentality provides me with the courage to be generous instead of selfish. It affords me peace at the airport when a flight is delayed. It dissolves self-doubt over my performance at work and affords me with greater teamwork with my coworkers. Abundance keeps me from over-investing emotionally in results and material possessions. It gives me confidence, trust, and security. I am able to approach others with love and generosity, be open, caring, and compassionate. It literally dissolves adversity and negativity.

The ego, on the other hand, is always trying to convince me to shift into a scarcity mindset as I start once again to think that I deserve more than others—that I am special and more important than they are and that I should get my fair share. When this happens, I feel greed, competition, envy, jealousy, and anger. In every waking moment of every day, I am either acting from a mindset of abundance or scarcity, and the outcome is directly attributable to that mindset. My level of happiness is based on my mindset of abundance or scarcity.

Abundance in four steps

By attracting into your life the unlimited abundance that is available to all of us, an abundance mentality has tremendous benefits on top of peace and lasting happiness. The law of attraction, which I referred to earlier, is real, and with practice you can attract into your life whatever it is you desire. By using the law of attraction, you can move from a position of need to a position of real intent. Intent is higher than desire as it connotes action and energy rather than just feelings of want. You can literally change your circumstances by shifting to an abundance mentality and practicing it through these four steps. I call this *experiencing abundance*. Have you ever heard anyone say, "I wanted it so bad I could taste it?" This is experiencing abundance; it is when your intent becomes so powerful that you can actually feel, taste, and smell it. When your desire becomes real intent, your subconscious aligns with your conscious, and you begin to attract to your life whatever you desire. The four steps of abundance are:

Step 1: Conceptualize what you need or want from an abundance mindset.

Step 2: Visualize step 1 in detail.

Step 3: Experience it.

Step 4: Surrender the outcome to God.

Although I have outlined a process that works for me, you may find that in many cases conceptualizing and visualizing is all you need to bring abundance into your life. At the same time, I don't want you to think that this is merely a technique, because techniques need to adapt as the situation changes. Abundance is a principle, a timeless and eternal principle, that when developed together and combined with integrity, compassion, and love will literally transform your life. This process will be rewarding beyond your ability to understand, and so you should accept it on faith and believe.

Beware that fixating and obsessing on the details can be dangerous. The danger in becoming attached and fixated on the exact outcome and specific details may bring disappointment. You need to find a balance between your intent and attachment to the results and timeline. It is quite likely that what you intend will be accomplished through miraculous events directed by God. When we become attached to the exact outcome, we become prescriptive and can miss the miracles that are right in front of us.

Step 1: Conceptualize. Convert and articulate your needs into positive desires and express them in an abundance mindset. This step of conceptualizing is the most critical step toward an abundance mentality. It is in this step that you actually shift your way of thinking from one of lack to one of abundance. You actually create the circumstances that you want to experience and actualize in your life. Going back to the example at the beginning of the chapter, if you are overweight, the shift to an abundance mindset is to express your real intent: This would mean saying, "I intend to eat healthy and exercise." Or you could say, "I see myself losing weight and being thinner." You actually create in your mind the scenario that will bring you health and your desired weight. Choose where you will exercise and what you will do. Another example may be that you hate your job. Transforming this desire to real intent is to say, "I intend to have a more satisfying job." Or, "I see myself working at ACME." You create a scenario where you actually see yourself in the job you desire. Articulate and conceptualize the scenario that you want to attract into your life.

Step 2: Visualize. Create a visual movie in your mind where you actually see yourself acting out the scenario that you have conceptualized. This is where you actually see yourself living an abundance mentality and create a mind-map of attraction. Whatever you see will be attracted into your life. Therefore, your visualization should be as detailed and specific as possible. If the scenario is to eat healthy, visualize yourself eating salads and vegetables. Envision yourself driving to the gym and exercising. Regarding the job scenario, visualize yourself doing the job that will bring you satisfaction. Visualize yourself doing the exact job that will be fulfilling to you. Visualize yourself being successful, meeting the people you will work with, seeing yourself with as much detail and realism as you can imagine. Spend a minimum of two minutes every day reliving this visualization. Don't let your visualization be wimpy. Make it grand, and think abundantly! Don't settle for just a mediocre lifestyle; visualize yourself as a new, thinner person working for a new company. Whatever you desire, make it a grand and exciting visualization. Your visualization has energy. As you visualize your intent, you will start to notice the energy that surrounds it. Energy that leads to miracles and that will bring your vision into existence.

Step 3: Experience abundance. Experience your visualization. Take your visualization and add the five senses—seeing, hearing, tasting, touching, and feeling—to it. This is when it becomes so real that you can taste it. This is when abundance comes to your life and brings your subconscious and conscious into alignment to transform your desires into intention with the full force of the law of attraction. You will experience miracles, which will bring to pass the things you have already experienced in this step. It may not be exactly as you have visualized it, but it will be close. Continue to practice this step until what you desire has been fulfilled.

Don't give up. Have patience and don't let self-defeating thoughts creep into your mind if things don't happen right away. Again, there is the temptation to become fixated on things happening the way you have seen and experienced them in step two. There is also the temptation to think that if what you are visualizing doesn't happen when you think it should, it must be wrong or it won't happen. God is not on your timetable. Stay the course. There is a mystery here—the mystery of how abundance unfolds. Let God unfold this abundance in your life.

Step 4: Surrender. Mentally and literally place your desires and intent in God's hands and let him work for you so you don't have to worry about it. This is an important step, as you will have the tendency to prescribe how your desires come to pass. God is more powerful than you or I. His ways are not our ways. If we attach ourselves to the outcome, we may miss the miracles that are about to take place. I am reminded of the story of a man stranded on the top of his house after a flood in the Midwest. A boat came by to rescue him, and he sent them on their way saying, "God told me he would save me come hell or high water. I am waiting for God to save me." Next, a helicopter came to lift him off the top of his house, and he responded in the same way. He was waiting for God to save him when all along he couldn't see that God was in fact saving him with the boat and the helicopter. He couldn't see this because he prescribed *how* God should save him. When it didn't happen how he prescribed, he couldn't see it.

You job is to conceptualize, visualize, and experience your intent. God's job is to accomplish it on your behalf or to reveal to you what it is you need to do. In the end, if you surrender to God, you will be amazed at the miracles that come into your life that help you to accomplish your real intent. The next chapter is dedicated to the principle of surrender where I expound on how you can make this a daily and continual practice.

There have been many scientific studies of people overcoming addictions, finding the ability to forgive, overcoming anger, overcoming cancer, and attracting enormous wealth into their lives through the steps I have outlined. I can't tell you exactly how an abundance mentality actually works. The unfolding of miracles is a mystery. All I can say is that it works. An abundance mentality has far-reaching effects on everything from personal relationships to business success to finance and wealth. You can live a life without limits, and you can have lasting happiness as you develop and practice abundance. Abundance mentality is not a mind-trick; it's not just positive thinking and affirmations. It is about real intent. It is about attracting into your life the abundance that God has for you—an abundance of happiness.

Practicing acceptance and an abundance mentality

Let's now put this chapter into action.

- Pick something that has been bothering you. It doesn't have to be the biggest or most important thing, but focus on it and then say, "It is what it is." Then decided to either accept it for what it is, extract yourself from it, or change it. Then follow through on your decision

- Get a notebook and set it at your bedside. Each night for the next twenty-one days, write down three things you are grateful for. This becomes your gratitude journal.

- Reach into your purse or your pocket. Pull out the first thing you touch. Look at it and be grateful for it. It might be a piece of candy, car keys, photos, or just a quarter. Truly look at it and express your gratitude for it. Then look at your immediate surroundings and be grateful for where you are, and then expand your view to be broader and do the same thing. You will find peace flow into you. Practice this every day.

- Now think of what it would be like to be happy in this moment. Keep that thought as you follow the steps to an abundance mentality:

  o Conceptualize it.

  o Visualize it.

  o Experience it.

  o Surrender it.

  o Do it again tomorrow.

Points to remember

- Redefine quality time to make it now time.

- The past and the future only exist in your mind. Now is real time.

- Multitasking is a myth.

- An abundance mentality attracts greater good into your life.

- There is no comparison.

- Have a gratitude attitude.

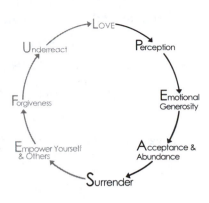

Chapter 5
Surrender

When you choose to surrender problems, adversity, challenges, and trials to God—you will find peace and happiness beyond what you can imagine. Instead of seeing problems and adversity everywhere, you will see opportunities to love.

Worry, stress, and concern are in opposition to happiness. The stress, concern, and worry you experience can be dissolved by the principle of surrender. The topic of surrender has been mentioned many times in the previous chapters as it relates to the miracle of a changed mind and perception as well as the fourth step to achieve an abundance mentality. We are familiar with surrender as often expressed as "I give up," or "I can't do this anymore," or simply, "whatever!" Surrender has other meanings ranging from resignation, acceptance of despair, or relinquishing to the power of another. It is the latter meaning that I would like to adopt here as a principle of the Happiness Factor. In this case, it is relinquishing to our higher power, to God. We typically think of surrender as giving up or failing. In the context of the Happiness Factor, surrender is positive. It is placing in God's hands what we do not control and giving to God those things that are an impediment to being happy.

The paradox is that in the giving we become more. We actually remove barriers to happiness and dissolve adversity and negativity through placing it all in God's hands as recognition that he is more powerful, more capable, more loving, and more able to deal with our life's challenges than we are. In essence, surrender is a turning away from the ego and a full adoption of our divine nature as our default nature. In order for that to happen, we need to "give up" or "surrender" aspects of the ego that have become second nature for us. It sounds easy, and it will be once you decide that you don't need to hang on to what does not bring you peace and satisfaction—when being at peace and being happy have a higher priority. We all have a comfort zone, and it could very well be that even things that are negative and destructive are comfortable to you because that is what you know. Surrendering those things may be a bit more difficult, but it is not impossible. This chapter is about giving up what keeps us from being happy. Surrender to be more kind, to be more compassionate, to be more loving, and to be happy.

Surrendering fear—becoming fearless

In October 1987, a 5.9-magnitude earthquake rocked Whittier, California. The epicenter was just ten miles from our house. My six-year-old daughter was standing in the kitchen when the quake hit, rattling our cupboards and dishes and causing a frightening noise that scared her terribly. She was not hurt physically, and we had no significant damage to our house, but she suffered severe emotional trauma. She clung to my wife not wanting to leave her side. She began to wet the bed, would not ride in elevators, and was having a hard time in school. It pained me to see my daughter so afraid and fearful of everyday things. If a door would slam, she would scream and run to find one of us. My heart was broken thinking that there was nothing I could do to help her. We tried counseling, we tried talking to her, we prayed for help and asked for blessings, but as the weeks went on, she continued to live in fear.

Several days later while sitting in traffic, I received a burst of inspiration. That evening Meghan and I wrote all of her fears on small pieces of paper and put them in a shoe box that we had decorated. It was the "fear box"—a box to put all of her fears in so she didn't have to be afraid anymore. Together we went into the garden, dug a deep hole, and buried the box of fears. From that moment on, Meghan had more courage and was less afraid. You could see it in her face, her posture, and hear it in her voice. Burying her fears in the garden was an outward expression of surrendering her fears and letting them go. Oh, to have the faith of a young girl trusting in her father to unburden and heal her. I can't take too much credit for what happened, because I was truly inspired. It was a miracle—a blessing from God.

We all have fears. I have fears. In fact, I have learned recently that I have more fear than I thought I did. My fears, typically expressed as anger, are stealthy and conniving, not wanting to be labeled or exposed. The ego loves fear, it relishes in you being afraid. Yet the fear is there, and unless, like my daughter, you find a way to let it go, it will continue to expose itself through misbehavior that hurts yourself and those around you.

We are all afraid of something, and most likely we have more fears than we care to admit. All of our actions and emotions can be defined as either love or fear. If we are not acting out of love, then we are demonstrating fear. It may not resemble more traditional fears such as being afraid of the dark or being afraid of heights, but it is fear nonetheless. Fear manifests itself in anger, greed, jealousy, or envy. Fear is also demonstrated by holding a grudge and being unwilling to forgive.

I am always amazed by the apparent fearlessness of young people. My youngest son is a competitive skateboarder ranked between second and fifth in the state for the past several years. I have a hard time watching him try new tricks, feeling my own fear of even getting on a skateboard. He appears fearless as he skates off a ten-foot ledge or jumps a long staircase. I asked him if he was afraid, and he admitted that he was always scared, but explained that if he let fear control him, he would never learn a new trick. Learning new tricks, he says, is what skating is all about. If my son can set aside his fear of landing face-first on the cement and not let fear control him, so can we. We can live a fearless life by surrendering our fears. Just like my son and daughter, when we surrender our fear, we live a life that is free from fearful limitations, empowering us to achieve a higher potential.

Whatever our fears, God is willing and capable of taking them from you. You simply need to offer them to him: "God, please take this fear from me. I am willing to be fearless in this situation and leave the outcome to you." A first step is to accept that you either operate from a position of love or fear. Any time you feel a negative emotion, you are feeling fear. Fear is the opposite of love, and surrendering it to God allows him to replace that fear with his love so that you are filled with love and happiness.

Surrendering the requirement of perfection

I was attending school for most of the first fourteen years of our marriage. Working full time and going to school full time left little time for my wife and family. Not to mention finding time for church assignments and the chores needed just to keep the household running. It seemed like I was in a constant state of stress and anxiety. Not that I was a nervous person, I felt I had too much to do and too little time to do it in. My wife's response would often be, "Kirk you need to go with the flow." But "going with the flow," was not for me—that was for slackers and hippies. Going with the flow was not my style.

I was a go-getter, a "take-action" kind of guy, and to me, to "go with the flow" was the equivalent of being lazy. But, like most things, she was right and I should have listened sooner. Tension and stress is often caused from an imaginary requirement that we need to be perfect to be happy or that an event or experience has to be perfect in order for us to feel happiness.

This isn't just for the religious; many of us have a high standard of perfection that is unrealistic and unobtainable, yet we continue to strive for it, only to be disappointed. For Christians and other churchgoers, the burden to be "perfect," unless kept in perspective, can create devastating guilt and depression. The requirement to be perfect is sometimes justified by verse 48 in the fifth chapter of Matthew, where in the Sermon on the Mount, Jesus says, "Be ye therefore perfect, even as your Father which is in heaven is perfect." But this verse can be taken in context with the five preceding verses where Jesus is expounding on the "perfect law of love." In that context, verse 48 can be interpreted as "be perfect in *love* as I and your Father in heaven are perfect in *love*." With the emphasis added to focus on love it makes more sense to me that what Jesus is saying is that in order to be like him, we must love. Giving up on your own standard of perfection means surrendering that energy to a higher power—the power that created the universe. I realize this may feel uncomfortable if you are a "dot the i's and cross the t's" kind of person. For many of us, we have been ingrained from an early age with the belief that anything less than perfection is a sin. This obsession with perfection is everywhere we turn and makes us think that we are not perfect if we aren't the right size, if we don't have the right hair color, if we aren't the right race, and so on. This just isn't so. Surrendering the need to be perfect is not about becoming a slacker, it's courageous. It's recognizing that we are who God has created, and it's a willingness to do what is necessary—to give up our obsession for perfection that brings so much pain and frustration. You are who God intended you to be just as you are, and your willingness to grow supports that.

The bottom line is that you do not need to be perfect. There have been times in my life when I felt the pressure to be perfect and that unless I achieved someone else's standard of perfection (like my parent's, children's or boss') I was a bad person for not living up to their ideals for me. In reality it was thinking I needed to please them that created the need to be perfect. I felt that by being more "perfect" I would be more accepted. Needing to be perfect was a standard I myself created, not something that was imposed upon me. Thoughts of perfection stem from feeling inferior and thus the need to please. An obsession to be perfect can also come from feeling superior, creating the need to demonstrate you are better than others think you are. Surrender your idea of perfection, surrender the need to please others, and you will find it has been a barrier to enjoying life and will lead to being happy.

Fishes and loaves: Surrendering our inadequacies and flaws

I love the Bible story where Jesus feeds the multitude of five thousand. Of all the different accounts in the Gospels, I prefer the one in chapter 6 of John, verses 1-14. You may recall that a multitude of people had followed Jesus to a mountain where he sat with his disciples. When he saw the multitude of people, he had compassion for them and asked Phillip, "Whence shall we buy bread that these may eat?" Phillip answers by saying that not even two hundred pennyworth of bread would be enough for every one of them to have even a small portion. Andrew must have overheard this exchange, for he said, "There is a lad here, which have five barley loaves and two small fishes: but what are they among so many?" Jesus then has the multitude sit in groups, and he takes the loaves and fishes, gives thanks, and gives them to the disciples to pass among the multitude to eat. When all was said and done, they collected what remained and filled twelve baskets with the fragments. Certainly five loaves and two fishes were inadequate for the task of feeding thousands of people. God, through his grace and power, made up the difference. How often are we faced with a task and feel inadequate, thinking we barely have the equivalent of five loaves and two fishes? We feel inadequate and berate ourselves for having so little to offer. However, if we would just surrender what we *do* have to God, he will make up the difference.

This is God's message to all of us: that it is more important to give what we have than to acquire what we don't have to please him. This story is more about what was going on inside the boy than what was going on around him. The same is true for us; when we focus our efforts and attentions on what is happening on the outside and forget about the inside, we are without peace and we are unhappy and full of contention. The outside cannot be controlled or predicted. We only have power over what is happening on the inside. It is through the atonement that God makes up the difference by compensating for inadequacies. The atonement is not just for sinners but also applies to our inadequacies, our inefficiencies and our character traits and flaws. When we do our part by giving to him our fishes and loaves, God will do his part. The small lad who gives the five loaves and two fishes is symbolic of us doing *all* we can in any given situation, and if there is more that is needed, we know that God will enlighten us, inspire us and guide us to do anything necessary to accomplish his will. This is surrender—leaving it to God and placing ourselves at his will to guide and direct us in doing what we can. That is our part.

In 1990 we moved from Whittier, California, to Boise, Idaho. We had outgrown our house in Southern California, and like many young families, we couldn't even afford to purchase the home we owned, so we relocated to Boise at a significant salary reduction. After a few years of increasing expenses on a smaller income, we were deeply in debt. Though we managed our money well, we were faced with student loan payments from law school coming due. I felt such financial desperation that bankruptcy seemed the only solution. Knowing I could not start the proceedings alone, I asked my wife to come with me to the attorney's office. She was dead set against bankruptcy as a matter of integrity and moral responsibility. Her message to me was, "You work hard, and you live a good life. Let God help us with this, and it will be okay. We don't need bankruptcy; we need a miracle." I was upset by her lack of support for what I felt was the right solution. I saw no way out—there was no way our income could support the debt we had accumulated and the loans that were coming due. We never made it to the attorney's office. I was forced to face my fear of debt, and that fear led me, mostly out of desperation, to God. I gave my debt to him; I surrendered to him the few loaves and fishes I had. It was inadequate—it was just a measly portion, and I felt that the loaves I was offering were unworthy, but I had no choice. Together, my wife and I were doing all we could. It was a difficult thing to do, knowing that the debt was due to our own actions, but we created it and needed to be responsible for it.

That night I surrendered all I had to God, and he took the burden from me. I felt at peace, and for the first time in several years, I felt unburdened from my financial woes and never worried about debt again. Something happened in the giving, in the surrendering, that gave me a greater capacity to manage our finances and to put a plan in place, leaving the rest to God. All I can say now is that it was a miracle that we were never contacted by creditors; we paid every bill, and in just a few years, we became debt free except for our mortgage. Without really knowing how, I had surrendered to God by acknowledging that his power is greater than mine—greater than all other powers. My attempt to control situations and people is actually a demonstration of distrust in God. My attempts to manage our budget and our debt led me to consider bankruptcy. God's solution for my debt was different. It was miraculous and allowed me to feel at peace and be happy even though the circumstances did not change. Through surrender, I became more than I was before; I had greater ability than I did before. I felt unburdened; I felt that God was my partner and that I was not alone. This brought peace, and I became happy.

In preparation for this book, I have spent a lot of time examining my life and where I have experienced unhappiness and contention instead of peace. As I considered all the times in my life when I was anxious and felt inadequate, I realized that these feelings occurred most often when I was trying to do it all on my own or when I was trying to please someone. There were other times that my own character flaws got in the way of my own peace as I hurt or disappointed those closest to me. Sure, I would pray and ask God for his help and his blessings, but instead of surrendering to him, I was prescribing what blessings I wanted by trying to control events, timelines, and, most often, other people. If I look back on the times when I worried the most, when I felt the worst, and I can see my worrying didn't do any good. It was an unproductive use of energy. Instead of drawing me closer to God, it actually separated me from him. More often than not, I would wonder why God was not listening to me, why he was not answering my prayers by giving me the blessings I was asking for and changing the people who were bothering me. All I needed to do was surrender to God what he had already given me—my fishes and loaves—and when I finally did, I had been transformed on the inside and able to receive more of his guidance and blessings. Just like the story in the Bible where Jesus' disciples gathered up the leftover bread filling twelve baskets with bread fragments, we end up being more than we were before and greater blessings come into our lives. Our inadequacies, inefficiencies, and flaws are no longer stumbling blocks to our happiness, we interact with people on a more peaceful level, we feel better about ourselves, and we are relieved of stress, worry, and anxiety. We can be happy.

Surrendering results

I am prescriptive and have been my whole life with a firm belief that anything is attainable if I work hard enough and live a life that is good enough. I love it when a plan comes together, especially a plan that I have devised. Most Saturdays I have a list of things that I want to accomplish, and the more I get done on that list, the better I feel about myself. As part of a church assignment, I watch over a few families in our congregation. For more than ten years, I have visited Cheryl at least once a month to share a spiritual message and to see if she has needs the congregation can fulfill. Cheryl loves her to-do list, which she masterfully creates each day. She also battles with a blood disorder that causes extreme fatigue. Her to-do list is created without the blood disorder in mind, and so on those days when the blood disorder is active, she is unable to accomplish her tasks in the time and in the way she had hoped. She becomes frustrated and anxious; as a result, the precious energy she needs to accomplish her tasks is used to deal with the frustration. The more frustrated she gets, the more energy she uses and the less she is able to accomplish. And so the days go on in a vicious circle until she crashes and needs bed rest to restore her energy. In a day or so, she feels good enough to create another to-do list, only to end up in bed several days later. After just a few cycles of this viscous circle, she becomes distraught, discouraged, self-blaming, and upset that she has a chronic disease. She is out of peace; she is unhappy, and she has little in the way of satisfaction.

Like many of us do, Cheryl attached herself to her tasks and the results of her to-do list. As long as things are going well, going as she has planned, she feels at peace, accomplished, and confident. When things don't go as she planned—if a task takes too long or if the blood disorder becomes active—her peace, satisfaction, and confidence disappear. Like Cheryl, we all attach ourselves to results and outcomes. As long as things go well we feel peace, satisfaction, and confidence. But these feelings are short-lived because very few things in life go as planned. While in Germany I have often heard the saying, "Der mensch denkt-Gott lenkt," which means, "Man plans, God laughs." Our own plans are no match for God's power and will. When things go well, it is oftentimes not because of us. Yet we consistently find ourselves in the same viscous cycle like Cheryl, trying to summon great powers to make things better using a brute-force mentality and thinking that if we just worked harder things would be better. Don't get me wrong here; I am in no way saying that we shouldn't work hard. I am saying we need to be mindful not to attach ourselves to the outcome. It is so easy to attach ourselves—our self-esteem, our confidence, our peace, and our happiness—to what we want to accomplish, and when it doesn't happen, the attachment fails and we fall apart. Our frustration and disappointment come from wanting to control and manipulate things we can't. The ego wants us to believe we can, so we find ourselves in the never-ending cycle of ups and downs, never finding peace, never finding lasting happiness. Robert Burns, the eighteenth century poet, coined the phrase "Even the best laid plans of mice and men often go awry." It is so true, and yet we continue to try and try and try.

Surrendering means giving up our attachment to *outward* results and placing them firmly in God's capable hands. We need to take an inside-out approach, becoming more concerned about what is happening on the inside and relax about what is happening on the outside.

This does not mean we don't strive for the best, that we don't work hard; it means we accept that God is in charge, that he is all powerful; that he is all loving; and that he will do what is best for everyone concerned, not just for me. It means that he will guide and inspire me to do what is needful and necessary. When I am firm in the knowledge that God knows and loves me, and I acknowledge his power and admit my helplessness, then I am no longer limited by envy, jealousy, and petty arguments. I am able to work more effectively and able to do so much more. He will do his part if I do mine. My part is to be an instrument in his hands and to leave the outcome to his will. In the Lord's Prayer found in the New Testament, Jesus says, "Thy will be done on earth as it is in heaven." This is not a conditional statement; I read it as a statement of fact. God's will be done on earth. Who are we to stand in the way of God's will? We are powerless and helpless, so why do we fight this so much when we could surrender ourselves to God's will and spend our efforts focusing on the inside, developing love rather than spending our efforts on results that are unpredictable at best. Surrendering results means we do our best and leave the rest to God. The idea that we are helpless and powerless has been hard for me to accept and at first I didn't agree. However, the more I practice surrender, the more I really consider my own power and abilities, I am convinced that I am no match for God's power and his will. He loves us and will do nothing that is not for our benefit.

Surrendering results requires faith in the power of God. Marianne Williamson puts it this way in her book *A Return to Love*: "Faith is an aspect of consciousness. We either have faith in fear or we have faith in love, faith in the power of the world or the power of God."[25] Faith exists; the question is whether your faith is in fear—afraid that things won't turn out the way you want—or whether your faith is in God — faith that he will do what is best for you. When we place our faith in

God, we surrender the outcome and the results, knowing that God will only act in the benefit of all concerned. We are unable to know what the outcome will be or how it will happen, but we don't need to. If we do our part, God will do his. God is like the masterful potter at the wheel, molding and managing the clay into something marvelous. Our attachment to the outcome and our attempts to control and manipulate events is like sticking our hands into the clay together with God's. With our hands in the way, it is harder for him to do his work and a big mess results. This creates extreme frustration for us. Let God do what he will with the clay; let his will be done.

Last year I introduced Cheryl to the concept of surrender. At first she was skeptical because she had placed her faith in her list and in her own strength. But as we worked on surrender, a miracle happened. In our last visit, she said something I thought I would never hear her say. When I asked how things were going, she said she was happy. For the first time in her life, she could honestly say that she was happy. Her circumstances had not changed, she had learned to surrender, and with surrender came peace and happiness.

Oprah Winfrey tells this story about surrender. She was obsessed with the book *The Color Purple* and would tell everyone about it. She even carried copies of the book with her and gave them to anyone who wanted one. Her dream was to be part of the movie and was willing to do almost anything from cleaning the set to playing a bit part; it didn't matter as long as she was part of making the movie. She was fortunate enough to audition for the part she eventually played, but it took courage to audition, and even more courage to wait for the decision. After auditioning she kept calling the casting agent to see if a decision had been made. She was told that there were others—other more famous actors—who had auditioned, and it would be a while until they made a final decision. After two months of waiting, Oprah went to a weight-loss spa. While she was walking the track, she surrendered the part in *The Color Purple* to God. She said, "God, I surrender this to you, and I am willing to be whatever you want me to be."[26] Almost the instant she said that, a worker called her to the telephone to speak to Steven Spielberg. Spielberg offered her the part and told her she couldn't lose one pound! As soon as she surrendered what she wanted most to God, the miracle happened for her. Surrendering results means surrendering the outcome, knowing that God is in charge and whatever the outcome, it will be for your benefit.

It is easier to surrender the things we really don't care much about, but surrendering means surrendering it all. The more important it is to us, the more important it is to surrender it to God. Surrender can start with a simple prayer, "God, I surrender this situation to you, knowing that through your love for me you will always have my best interest in mind. I am willing to do my part. Help me to love, help me to have compassion, help me to see things as you would see them. If there is something I need to do, even if it is hard, even if it is uncomfortable, I am willing to do it. I place this in your hands."

You can surrender anything in any situation. I start my day by surrendering my to-do list to God, going over each item and placing it in God's hands and asking for the inspiration and courage to do all things with love and with his guidance. I then go over each appointment in my calendar and surrender those meetings as well. During the day, I may need to surrender feelings, emotions, and desires to God, and in so doing, I find greater effectiveness and productivity. I find that I am less distracted by the drama of life and able to focus on what matters most. There is great confidence in knowing that a great power is at work here and that God is my partner through the day and in all things. This confidence brings me peace that leads me to be happy.

Surrendering the need to be right

In any given situation, there are multiple versions of the truth. On an empirical and intellectual level, we probably all believe that each person sees things differently but are unwilling to admit that we might be wrong. On an emotional level, however, we hang on to the need to be right at the expense of our own peace of mind. Why does being right feel so good? The ego loves the feeling of being right, but even more so the ego wants others to know that they are wrong. The ego convinces you that there is a master scorecard on which you can win points by being right and bonus points when others know they are wrong. Living life based on keeping score creates a never-ending battle of competition in a game that cannot be won. We attach ourselves to being right the same way we attach ourselves to results and outcome. For some, being right is necessary for their self-value and confidence. You will know this person by how often he says, "I told you so." No one likes to hear "I told you so," but we love to say it. It doesn't even need to be said word-for-word because our body language and other verbal remarks imply it. For those of us hearing it, we don't hear it exactly as it is said. We usually hear something like, "I told you so, DUMMY," or "I knew this would happen; you are so stupid." The need to be right can destroy relationships and careers.

The more I mature, the more I begin to believe in the uncertainty principle. I don't mean the quantum physics principle of uncertainty but my own uncertainty principle: *the more certain I am, the more certain I can be that I am uncertain.* Or to put it in plain language: there is no way I can be right more than 50 percent of the time. There is just as much chance of being wrong as there is being right. Being right all the time carries with it a huge burden—the burden of defending your position, the burden of criticism from others, and the burden of contention. Not to mention the fact that when people think you are a "know it all," they don't want to be around you. When you acknowledge that you are powerless compared to your higher power, the importance of being right disappears and is replaced by a natural sense of curiosity. In many cases, you learn more than you ever thought you could, including that you are not right as often as you thought. I have discovered the more I say "I don't know," the more I learn and the better relationships I have. Admitting you don't know anything puts you in a position to learn everything. Surrendering the need to be right is simply stating that you are *willing to consider* that the other person might be right. Think of all the arguments you've had with your spouse or partner that could be dissolved by saying, "I am not saying you're right, but I am willing to *consider* that you are right." That short statement alone removes contention and allows a deeper and more effective discussion. This is not just true at home, but at work as well.

Not long ago, my wife and I were in counseling, and for several sessions, we argued over past events and over whose interpretation of the event was right. We were stuck in this catch-22 of judging each other's behavior while only considering our own intent. When I finally learned to surrender the need to be right by saying things like, "Oh, is that how you saw it?" or "You could be right," we began to make progress and get beyond the arguing of right or wrong to identifying the real issues. There are many times we subconsciously sabotage discussions and confrontations by arguing about who is right so we don't have to address the real issue. Often we reject feedback from someone because we just can't accept that he or she may be right. Your spouse may say that you are angry all the time, and a friend may say you smoke too much or that you don't return phone calls. Being willing to consider that they may be right can open your eyes to valuable feedback that will enable you grow and improve.

Again, surrendering the need to be right can be expressed in this way: "I am willing to consider that you may be right." You can't believe the magic those words have. I have felt a burden lift off my shoulders by just letting go of the need to be right and giving that to God. You can say to God, "I am unable to know who is right, but I am willing to consider that I am wrong. I give this to you; I surrender this to you, and I will let you make it right in your eyes. Bless me with the courage to admit that I might be wrong, and guide me to what is right." You will find that being right is no longer as important as being happy.

Surrendering the past and the future

Not only may we be attached to results and have a strong need to be right, we may still be hanging on to the past. At the same time, we may feel stress and anxiety regarding the future. Throughout the book I refer to the fact that the past only lives on in your mind. This is a significant point, as I have found that many people hang on to the past for better or worse. Having a realistic view regarding the importance of past events is essential to being happy. If you hold on to the past too tightly, you are attaching yourself to the past, and it can remove you from the happiness that is available to you in the present. Sure, the past may not be negative, and you could instead have fond memories of the past and long for the "good ol' days." Either way, you are attaching yourself to the past. The past and future only exist in your mind and need to have the proper perspective and importance that I have covered in previous sections. This section focuses on surrendering your attachment with the past and the future so that the present can be free from baggage and distraction.

When you accept and acknowledge that there is a power greater than you, you make a powerful admission that you are what God has intended—that all that has happened to you has made you who you are today. This admission can have a powerful transforming effect. The fact that my mother abandoned me at an early age could be the best excuse for almost anything. Think of it—I could do almost anything and blame it on abandonment issues and everyone would understand. They certainly would not agree, but they could understand. I could become addicted to drugs, alcohol, or just be lazy, always giving the excuse that I was abandoned. I could blame my anger, my fear, and all that is wrong with me on my mother. I am sure many of you could do the same. No one comes from a fully functional family. Don't think for a minute that you are excused from anything because your family or your parents were dysfunctional or because you were abandoned. It is simply part of the past, which you can learn from and become a greater and better person because of it.

God was present in the past, and if you look carefully, you will see his hand in your life. I am ultimately grateful that my mother abandoned me. The positives far outweigh the negatives. Was it hard, you bet! But I am more independent, a harder worker, and I have a greater sense of family and unity than I would have had otherwise. It was not my fault that she left, and when I consider it, I can't even imagine the stress and conflict she must have felt in leaving. Surrendering my mother's abandonment has allowed me to feel free and complete. My relationship with my mother has never been better, and I am so glad that she is in my life. I could not have felt as whole or complete if I had not surrendered the past to God. Lucinda Bassett, in her book *From Panic to Power*, says this: "No matter what your background, if you started with low self-esteem or low self-confidence, it can work for you or against you, depending on how you utilize the experiences in your life."[27] Surrendering your past to God, doing your part so he can do his, will allow you to see your past differently and allow you to draw power from it rather than it depleting power from you.

God will lead you from this present point into the future. Many of us are plagued with anticipatory anxiety. This anxiety can be related to fear about an upcoming event or worry over something or someone. No one but God can predict the future. There is no healing in the future; healing and power only exist in the present. You can surrender the future to God just as you surrender the past. Most often, what we believe can happen and what we worry about is never as bad as what we think and most likely doesn't happen at all. We can surrender all situations and future events to God. If we do our part, he will do his. You don't need to worry about the future. We need to be mindful of the future but turn the worry and the unfolding of events over to God with the assurance that it will be for our greater good.

Children, family, relationships

The people we love and feel closest to are oftentimes the ones we have the hardest time with and can hurt us the most. Too often our desire is for them to change so that they won't hurt us any longer. We hope, wish, and even pray that our parents, spouse, bother, sister, or others change so we can have peace, and when they don't change, we resent them or try to change them ourselves. Maybe we are concerned over a wayward child and feel guilt, remorse, and pain over their poor choices. No matter how hard you try, you cannot make anyone change. People only do what they want to do or they do it against their will, which results in resentment and anger toward you. We cannot change anyone; we can only change ourselves, and that is hard enough without having to worry about others. Your pain may not come from a relationship, but from the lack of a relationship in which you feel abandoned physically or emotionally. As much as you might try, you cannot make someone love you—you cannot make them believe what you believe, nor can you make someone who has abandoned you return to your life. All of this pain can be surrendered to God, and then you can let his will be done.

Kris and Sam are active in their church and congregation, but not every one of their children attends church or participates actively in a congregation. They don't fully agree with their choices, professions, or lifestyles. I am sure many of you experience the same situation where a child has strayed from the values and morals you tried to raise them with. You long for a loving relationship with them, but the gap is so wide and deep that you doubt it will ever be breached.

Perhaps your relationship with your son or daughter has degraded to an abusive or even violent state. Your heart is broken, and you long for the return of that little child you loved so much and had so many hopes and dreams for. You feel powerless and helpless to heal the relationship. You may even question how God, who loves all children, can allow your child to be lost. Acknowledging a higher power and surrendering to him means surrendering those relationships that mean the most to us. Our attempts to control and manipulate others to our own way of thinking or to make someone love us cannot succeed. When we surrender these relationships to God, we acknowledge that his love for our children is greater than our love for them. We submit that he is more powerful than we are. My children are his children, and I am merely an earthly host for them. God loves his children and gives us the opportunity to love them as well. I have surrendered my relationships with my children, my spouse, my family, and others to God, knowing that if I do my part, he will do his part. My part in any relationship is to accept what is and love. For me, that means that my relationship with my children is more important than anything they have done, anything they have said, or anywhere they have gone. It is more important that I love my children as God would love them than turn my back on them. It also means that I can surrender worry and guilt as well. Maybe you think you weren't as good a mother or father as you wanted to be, or maybe you blame yourself for how and where your child is right now. Surrender all of that to God and make love the only ingredient in any relationship. This will enable God's power to work on your relationships and develop them according to his will. God will not compel someone to act a certain way, even if it is for their own benefit.

Our prayers for our children should not be a request for God to make them act exactly how we want them to or to make them believe a certain thing. My prayers for my children have changed drastically over the past few years. Instead of pleading with God to have them believe or act a as I want them to, I pray they will acknowledge God, accept his power into their lives, and surrender to him. When surrender happens, all else that is good will come into focus.

Not that long ago, my wife and I were returning from downtown Boise and discussing our eldest son, lamenting his choices and his lack of a steady job. We were imposing our judgment upon him, wishing he would embrace our beliefs and values. As we were driving, we noticed a dirty beat up car a few cars in front of us making a left turn. The car was lurching, barely able to make it through the intersection. Drivers were irritated and angry, and many people honked their horns and used hand gestures. My wife and I watched from a few cars back as the driver got out of the car and opened the hood. She was haggard, poorly dressed, and unkempt, matching the car she was driving. The car directly behind her quickly pulled over, and a young man got out of his car to help. My wife and I were touched by the kind gesture of someone stopping to help this woman. The light changed and we turned left watching closely the scene on the side of the road. As we passed, we saw that the young man helping this woman was our son—the son we were just lamenting over and judging. It was like a slap in the face. I immediately felt bad about how I had judged my own son. I know many church-going and God-fearing people who wouldn't have stopped to help this woman. I am not sure I would have stopped to help her, and yet, here was my own son doing something so kind and loving.

My prayers for my son changed that day, and I began asking that I learn from him and that I see him the way God does. I started to pray that goodness would abound in his life and that he would have the courage to live a life of integrity and love. I surrendered my relationship with my son to God, knowing that God loves him more than I ever could and that he is in good hands. At the end of the day, my ability to love has more to do with the health of my own relationship with God than anything else. It isn't really about my relationship with my spouse, my children, my father, mother, or friends; it is about my relationship with God. As I learn to love and seek love in any and every situation, I have found that I don't even need to worry or be concerned about my relationships with others. The hurt, the pain, the guilt, remorse, and judgment have all dissolved. As I live the life God would have me live, when I focus on the inside and surrender the outside to God, all of my relationships improve. If you are feeling a separation in any relationship—if you feel contention, if you feel abandoned—the only relationship you need to worry about is your relationship to God. As you live a loving, compassionate, and kind life, miracles will happen, your relationships will mend, and you will be happy and at peace.

Surrendering problems and adversity

Now we come to a key aspect of the Happiness Factor, where all of our problems, negativity, adversity, and challenges can be dissolved. We all have problems and adversity, and I meet people every day in every city I visit who have real problems. From being abandoned by my mother, to cancer, extreme debt, and unemployment, I have had my share. The one conclusion I have come to is that I can no longer judge the difference between a problem and a blessing. While the timing and the intensity may differ, the result is typically the same—my problems, my trials, my adversity have all been blessings. It can be the same for you.

When I look back on it now, having cancer was such a growth opportunity for me; I am a better person for having had cancer. Having been abandoned, and not having a relationship with my mother for so many years, does not lessen who I am but has made me a better man. My friends Joe and Sue, whose son and daughter have Friedriech's Ataxia, admit that it has been one of the greatest blessings in their lives. Problems *only* exist in your own frame of mind. For God, all things are for your good and benefit. If all things are for your good, then all things are a blessing, and there are no problems or adversity to speak of. Your question should no longer be "Why is this happening *to* me?" but "Why is this happening *for* me?" God knows what he is doing! He is directing my life, and when I let him lead, I will be taken care of. Many of you know Psalms 23 and perhaps have committed it to memory. Now is the time to imprint it in your heart as well. When you acknowledge and surrender to God and let him lead, you shall not want, and he will take on all your burdens. When we do our part, he will do his part. Our part is to choose love in every situation and every circumstance. As you surrender your problems, adversity, challenges and trials to God, you will find peace and happiness beyond what you can imagine. Instead of seeing problems and adversity everywhere, you will see opportunities to love.

Consider two sailboats on a wide channel of water heading in opposite directions, both praying for wind to speed them on their journey. How does God answer those prayers? Providing the best wind for one will harm the other. If you were one of the captains praying for wind at your back, and yet the wind was blowing into your face, you might think that God has abandoned you and that he is punishing you. You might think you had a real problem and even question your self-worth.

127

If the wind is at your back with smooth sailing, you might determine that God is great and feel the warmth of a marvelous blessing. God operates for the greater good of all concerned. All problems are solved from the inside, not the outside. Your surrendering is the desire to capture whatever wind God provides and be the best captain of your boat that he will allow. When you start to see problems, it is a signal that you need to surrender.

You are not your problems. Your trials, negativity, and adversity or circumstances do not define who you are. We all have problems; we all have trials and challenges as part of being human and living on this earth. The difference is learning how to partner with God so he can worry so you don't have to. There is a miracle waiting for you when you surrender what bothers you most, what challenges you most, what causes you the most stress, concern and pain. Give it to God and be happy.

You are not alone

In order for surrender to be effective at least two things must happen. You must first acknowledge that there is a higher power—a greater force in the universe that created all things and provides all things. This power created you and instilled you with divine nature and the ability and capability to love. Look around you. All you see was created by this power—the plants that provide oxygen and the sun that warms you and provides light and energy. I define this higher power as God. You may believe this power originates from another source, and you may call it by a different name. Regardless, this higher power is available to each of us and is poured out upon all things, situations, and creatures without condition. The acceptance and acknowledgement of this higher power is essential to bring you peace and happiness through surrender. Secondly, you must admit that *without* this higher power, you are powerless. You must admit to being helpless and incapable of controlling people, events, and situations. This admission enables you to call upon your higher power and say to him, "I turn this situation over to you because I am unable to solve this. I know you love me; you will only do what is best for me and for all involved. I surrender this to you." Through surrender we allow God to be our partner in all we do, not just in times of crisis or extreme need, but every day and every moment.

When I was a young boy we had a sleepover in our back yard. There were seven of us, and we each had friends over to spend the night. There must have been at least fifteen kids sleeping in the back yard. In the middle of the night, I was kidnapped by four men who carried me away from my house. Fortunately they dropped me and took off running. I too ran. I ran back to my house and went immediately to my father. At first he did not believe that I had been kidnapped, but he finally came with me into the backyard. The four men, now looking more like boys, were there! They were all laughing and having a good time. My father rushed out the back door and caught two of the boys before they could escape. I can't remember what my father did or what he said, all I can remember is the strong sense of security knowing that my dad took care of it. Surrendering to God is the same thing. We can have a strong sense of security and confidence that God will take care of whatever we surrender to him. I am not sure what would have happened if I had not gone straight to my father. I could not have controlled the situation like he did; I could not have caught them before they escaped, but my father did. Our Father can, and he will. All you have to do is surrender to his higher power and then relax, let God be your partner. You are not alone.

My struggle has not been with the acknowledgement of God's existence and his love. My struggle has been with the admission that

I am helpless, because I have always taken pride in my ability to get things done, my intellect, and my work ethic. Admitting that I am helpless made me feel that all my gifts, talents, and strengths were for naught. What would I be without my skills, talents, and abilities? I thought I would be nothing, so I resisted the required admission of being powerless and helpless. We have all heard people say, "I am nothing without my God." I used to scorn at that. Now, however, I understand and accept it. In effect, I was turning my back on God by not trusting in his power and love, which is so much greater than I can even imagine. There are so many people who need to hit rock bottom to realize that they are powerless and that God's power is all there is. But you don't have to hit rock bottom; you can start to acknowledge that you are powerless over the problems you face today. Admitting that you are powerless and helpless is an acknowledgement that you are willing to accept God as your all-powerful, all-knowing, all-loving partner in every situation and circumstance.

When I finally admitted that I am powerless and surrendered to God, an unbelievable burden lifted off my shoulders. It was as if I no longer had to bear the world's burdens on my own. As the burdens lifted, I was able to see more clearly. Imagine a basket of burdens on your back so heavy that to carry the load you have to hunch over, only able to see the rocky ground you are walking on. God lifted that basket of burdens off my back, and I was able to stand up straight and see the beauty and light all around me as if for the first time. Surrendering does not mean that I am now on the proverbial easy street; it means that I will be more effective by not having to worry about the outcome. Surrendering means doing the best you can. I now regularly visualize turning over my burdens to God. I actually create a visual basket with my burdens in it and offer it to God. He willingly takes it.

Recently, we decided to relocate from Idaho to Arizona and were forced to sell our home in a slow market. Having enlisted a realtor and cleaned and prepared the house for sale, I then visualized myself walking in a quiet and beautiful garden. In this garden, God was sitting on a bench near a fountain of pure water. In my hands, I held a miniature replica of our house. I approached the bench where God was sitting, and as I came close, he stood up and embraced me in his arms. He said to me, "I am so glad you brought your house to me." I said to him, "We have done all we can do, there are so many variables and events that need to happen to sell our house that I am powerless to do them. I surrender the sale of our house to you, knowing that you will only do what is best for me and my family. If there is anything more I can do, I am willing. Just let me know." In my mind, I saw him accept the miniature model of my house as if I had given him a precious gift. He looked me in the eye and said, "You don't need to worry about this. I will take care of it. You will know if I need you to do anything." We embraced, and I thanked him with all the tenderness I could express and retreated from the garden.

Was my part done? No, we still needed to keep the house clean, fix any repairs, and make the house available for showing. We still needed to do our part. It was a slow real estate market—probably not the best time to sell a house. But neither my wife nor I felt anything but peace. We knew God loved us—that he would take care of us and that we were unable to understand or control all the events necessary to sell the house. We knew that our house would sell when God willed it—and it did. We had two full-price offers, and we believe it was a miracle. Again, when you truly acknowledge the higher power of God and your own powerlessness, you allow God to be your partner, and he will do the heavy lifting for you. Your surrender literally dissolves worry, stress, and anxiety, bringing you peace to be happy.

Practicing surrender

- Consider one of the things you don't like about yourself. Now give this flaw, this inadequacy, this concern to God.

- What is one thing you are fearful of? Not being good enough, not having enough money, losing your job—what ever it is—give it to God and pledge to do your part. Surrender your fears by saying: "God, please take this fear from me. I am willing to be fearless in this situation and leave the outcome to you,"

- Set your to-do list in front of you—now go over each item and surrender it to God. Let him be your partner.

- Look at yourself in a mirror and accept and internalize that you do not need to be perfect, and surrender your idea of perfection. You are who God intended, and God loves who you are and will guide you to be better.

Points to remember

- Fishes and loaves: surrendering what we have—even when it isn't enough, even our own inadequacies and character flaws—gives God the permission to make up the difference, and we become more.

- Surrender your need to be right. You can say to God, "I am unable to know who is right, but I am willing to consider that I am wrong. I give this to you, I surrender this to you, and I will let you make it all right in your eyes."

- Surrender both the past and the future. The past cannot harm us. If we do our part, he will do his. Be mindful of the future, but turn the worry and the unfolding of events over to God.

- Focus on your relationship with God—be kind, compassionate, and loving and all other relationships will heal themselves.

- Acknowledge the higher power of God and your own powerlessness. This allows God to be your partner, and he will do the heavy lifting for you. Your surrender literally dissolves worry, stress, and anxiety, bringing you peace and happiness.

Chapter 6

Empowering yourself and others to be happy

One of the best things we can do for those around us is to live happily. As we do this, we empower them to be happy. Just like the ripples in a pond when a stone is cast into the water, the happiness we feel has an effect on others.

Most people do not believe they have any control over whether they are happy or not. Their comments have lead me to believe that they expect happiness to just happen and that one day when things are just right, they will finally be happy. The ego wants us to believe that we have no control over whether we are happy, and so it convinces us that happiness is found in material accumulation. Being happy is the one thing you have control over more than anything else, because it is something you can choose. We each have the power to be happy, and by making that choice, we become empowered to be happy regardless of the circumstances. With the choice to be happy, we also empower those around us to be happy as well.

Many people I meet are discouraged in their effort to be happy. They fill their life with serving and doing the right things but have yet to experience satisfaction and fulfillment. For instance, Rachel recently joined a church after feeling there was something missing in her life. The more she goes to church, the more inadequate she feels, as she finds so much she needs to improve to be religious. She is discouraged in thinking that maybe she doesn't have enough faith. Going to church should make you happy, right? What about Jake? He is overwhelmed by all the people he has to care for—his elderly mother, his brother that does not have a job, and friends that are always calling for him to come do this or that. He is serving them, and service should bring happiness. Right? Abbey knows that when she finally has done all she can, God will help her. It is hard for her to know when she has done all she can because there is always more she could and should do. She is constantly trying to reach the point where God will step in and make her happy.

I too had spent a long time waiting to be happy when all along I had the power to be happy no matter what. For most of my life, I felt that I needed to demonstrate a high degree of self-reliance and needed to do all I could before God would do his part. I felt constant conflict between self-reliance and trusting God with all my heart, mind, and strength. I questioned how I could fully rely upon God and still do all I needed to do, thinking that trust in God and self-reliance were separate. I have since learned that they are mutually inclusive, not mutually exclusive. I erred in defining my role by thinking I needed to bring more than five loaves and two fishes to the table. It is not what we bring to the table that matters; it is what is on the inside that matters most. As we start to identify more with our divine nature, our conscience then becomes a valued guide in doing right for the right reasons. Identifying with our divine nature and following our conscience empowers us to be happy. This does not mean that we can just sit back and do nothing; it means relaxing and acknowledging that God is in control. We no longer need to waste emotion or energy trying to control things and people, because we can't.

The Happiness Factor empowers us to do our part more effectively so that God can do his part. Doing our part may require us to do things that are hard, things that are uncomfortable, things that are outside our comfort zone. The difference is that we are now empowered by having God as our ultimate partner in accomplishing what we intend. It is the worry and the anxiety that we no longer need to experience as we do our part. Worry and anxiety can enter our life when we stray from our moral code and follow the ego instead of our conscience. Our conscience is God speaking to us through the Holy Spirit. As we follow the conscience, we align with God and become true to our divine nature, empowering us to now go forward with full faith and knowing that God will only do what is best for us. Our part is to be an instrument in God's hands, knowing that no matter what happens it will be for our own good. Just like a saxophone is only formed metal until air is blown through it, we too are only instruments in God's hands becoming empowered and effective as we do his will. I have learned that when I am aligned with God's will, putting a priority on kindness, compassion, love, and integrity and doing the right thing for the right reasons, happiness happens. Being happy is not about being a contented couch potato, it is taking an active and more effective role and taking responsibility for your inner peace by doing what God inspires you to do. Inspiration is the essence of empowerment and works the same way a car works—you cannot steer a car if you are not moving. God is willing and able to steer for us, but we need to start moving. That is our part, we need to act, to start moving, and God will guide and direct us if we let him. Looking back, I can now see that previously I was using God for *my* benefit rather than letting him use me for *his* benefit. How do we maintain identity with our divine nature when the social conscience demands that we follow the ego? This chapter will help you discover how to do that.

Your own happiness is like a pebble in a pond, sending ripples of happiness and peace that are felt by those around you. Research by University of Warwick researcher Nick Powdthavee reveals that married men and women are significantly more satisfied with their lives when their partner is satisfied with life. [28] This study analyzed data from more than nine thousand married individuals in the British Household Panel Survey (1996–2000 and 2002) on how married couples rated their satisfaction with life over a multiyear period. The analysis showed that as one partner's satisfaction increases, the other's satisfaction increases as well. In fact, they found that the satisfaction of one partner can overcome the negative aspects of the other partner losing their job or getting ill. The opposite is also true where one partner's satisfaction in life decreases, so does the other's. This leads me to conclude that one of the best things we can do for those around us is to live happily, and as we do this, we empower them to be happy. The ripple effect of our happiness has an impact on those around us.

There is a law of attraction here that as we think positively and live happily, we will attract that into our lives. In his book *Power vs. Force: The Hidden Determinants of Human Behavior*, David R. Hawkins finds that both as an individual and as a community, our positive thoughts and happy living have a positive impact on entire populations and can counterbalance the negativity of the sad events we see in the news each day. [29]

There is a famous saying that goes like this: "Give a man a fish and you feed him for a day. Teach a man to fish and you feed him for a lifetime." Sharing the points in this book will help you teach someone how to fish; you empower them to take responsibility for their own happiness. As I have shared these concepts with my family and friends, I have witnessed them grow in happiness and live more satisfying lives. I have felt more connected with them, and I have seen their confidence to face life's challenges increase. I am witnessing them become empowered to be happy.

Doing your part

If you were on a deserted island would you be happy? Not likely. But I am sure there are days you wish you were alone on a deserted island. We must interact with the people and the world around us. These people, most with good intentions, may be expecting you to solve their problems. They may expect you to be responsible for their satisfaction, contentment, and happiness. Worse yet, they may blame you for their unhappiness. It is even possible that people around you will shun your attempts to be happy, thinking that if they can't be happy then no one can. I am not saying that they are out to sabotage your happiness on purpose, but if they are listening to the ego and allowing it control their lives, their thoughts and actions will cause it to seem that way.

Who is it you have the most trouble with? Who is your biggest pain? I am sure that as I ask that question at least one and maybe more than one person comes to mind. Have you ever played the hot potato game? I remember this game from when I was young. In this game, we would stand in a circle and pass around an object we called the "hot potato." The object of the game is to pass the "hot potato" to the person next to you as soon as you can so as not to be caught with the potato when the game stops. Our interaction with others is sometimes like this game of hot-potato, where people around us want to pass their burdens on to us. When this happens, we are challenged to find joy and peace in the relationship as it deteriorates to one of obligation and need. There are so many people who have lost peace by taking on the "hot potatoes" that their family, friends, coworkers, and children throw at them. I like this analogy because when we take on someone else's problems, we start to feel pain and lose peace just as if we held a hot potato in our hands.

You have a choice; you can take the potato and burn your hands, or you can empower them by helping them learn how to handle hot potatoes themselves. We may be tempted to blame the other person for manipulating us into dealing with their problems when the truth is that we have trained them to be that way. As we engage with the people around us, we actually train them how to treat and manipulate us. For those of you holding the hot potatoes of your family, friends, children, and others, it is time to gently pass it back and empower them to hold on to it. You don't have to lose peace and you don't have to take on the burdens of others. Rather, you can pass it back to them with compassion, kindness, and love. When we act with love, compassion, kindness, emotional generosity, and the other points in this book, we are actually empowering those around us to be happy as well.

"Sure," you say, "but where do I draw the line? How do I actually do that?" Having compassion for the burdens and concerns of those around you without taking those burdens on as your own requires courage and strength. Let me help you develop this courage and strength. At its core, this strength is developed by an unwavering knowledge and commitment that you are not responsible for anyone else's happiness. At first this may be hard for you to accept and may be contrary to your personal and religious philosophy, especially if you have lived your life thinking that you are supposed to please others and make them be happy. But you can't. You cannot make anyone happy. You cannot please anyone enough to make them happy. What, then, is your responsibility? Your responsibility is to treat all people with love and compassion.

There is a difference between serving someone and trying to please them to make them happy. If you do something in an effort to please, the ego demands compensation in the form of recognition. When you don't get the recognition you feel you deserve, you feel resentment. Start now to recognize whether you are serving out of love or trying to please.

When you try to please, you take on the responsibility for someone else's happiness, and whether it is your spouse, your children, your mother, your father, or your siblings, you are actually doing them a disservice by preventing them from learning how to be happy themselves.

I know this is easier said than done. Not only will it take practice, you might also experience some resistance from those you have been pleasing. I am not suggesting you turn your back on people you have felt the need to please but to ask God to help you see the relationship differently and give you the strength and courage to love them. Here is a simple prayer to help you. "Dear God, help me recognize when I do something to please rather than to serve with love. Grant me the courage to kindly resist trying to make someone happy and serve them instead with love." The key indicator is your own level of peace. If you are not at peace, then you either need to change how you perceive the person, lovingly decline, or lovingly serve them.

I love the story of the Good Samaritan found in the New Testament. The story of the Good Samaritan is an excellent blueprint for how we can approach those in need without taking their burdens upon us or trying to please. In Luke, chapter 10, Jesus recounts a parable about a man who, traveling from Jerusalem on the way to Jericho, fell among thieves who steal his clothes, wound him, and leave him for dead on the side of the road. Later, a priest sees the stricken man and avoids him, passing to the other side of the road, presumably in order to maintain ritual purity. Similarly, a Levite, seeing the man wounded and dying, ignores him as well. Then a Samaritan notices the injured man and, despite the mutual animosity between Samaritans and the Jewish population, has compassion for him and immediately renders assistance by binding his wounds, setting him on his donkey, and taking him to an inn to recover while promising to cover the expenses. He pays the innkeeper in silver coins equal to an entire day's wages for an average laborer and tells the innkeeper that he will return and pay for any further care the wounded man needs.

For years, I had read this story and heard it in various sermons and lessons. But it wasn't until recently that I was able to read between the lines and see that the Samaritan gave compassionate and "adequate" service. The concept of adequate service is difficult because each situation is different, and some situations require urgent and immediate assistance. The Good Samaritan took adequate care of the man in need, but you don't read that he sold his farm or quit his job or moved his family closer to the wounded and injured man. Nor did he pack up the man's things and give him a room in his house. He arranged for his care, checked up on him, and blessed him as he departed.

I have had many conversations with clients battling resentment for being "manipulated" into helping others with things they should be doing themselves; where caring for someone or doing things for them has become a tremendous physical, emotional, and financial burden. Where once there was satisfaction and joy in service, it has now become a source of stress, contention, and anger. Seeing someone as needy is just that—it is the way you see them, it is a judgment. Ask God to change your mind about the person, ask to see them in their innocence, and you will no longer experience them as needy and feel the need to please them. As I have worked on this with various clients, an amazing transformation has taken place. They have suspended judgment about who they are serving and started to see them the way God sees them. They begin to place love above all else and no longer see people as needy. Their neediness literally disappears and turns into an opportunity to love, and they literally become the miracle in the lives of the people they are serving. You have the opportunity to "be the miracle" by serving others. Surrender the situation to God, ask for his guidance in serving, and you will be amazed at your capacity to render adequate service, rather than pleasing, to make someone happy. By doing this, you stay within peace and can be happy as you do well for others. Be the miracle—be happy.

Spirituality, religion, and happiness

There is a difference between spirituality and religion. Not everyone who is religious is spiritual, and not everyone who is spiritual is religious. I have witnessed many people find religion and have seen many people become spiritual. Regardless of which you pursue, you can become closer to your maker and enrich your life. In fact, studies have shown that people who have a religion and do their best to live the values of that religion are more content than those who do not.[30]

Personally, I have found that spirituality does not *automatically* lead to happiness. Though I have always taken my spirituality and my religion seriously, there was something missing. It was as if I had a checklist of things I had to do to be spiritual, and as I checked things off the list, I became more spiritual but not necessarily happier. In becoming spiritual, I wanted to live a life free of resentment and contempt for my fellow man. Yet there was something missing. Paul the apostle expresses similar sentiment in 1 Corinthians 13. In this chapter, Paul enumerates several aspects of spirituality: speaking as an angel, prophesying, speaking in tongues, and having faith enough to move mountains. According to Paul, these are all aspects of spirituality. Yet he also says that it is not enough—that without charity it will all be for nothing. It is not *what* we do as much as *how* and *why* we do it because charity is found on the inside, not in what we do on the outside. Charity is the "pure love of Christ." I like to think of it as the same love that Christ would have for any person in any circumstance. It is the love we have as we identify with our divine nature. Charity has been defined as love, benevolence, and good will. It is a disposition of heart that inclines men to think favorably of their fellow men and to do them good. In essence, it is the highest, noblest, strongest kind of love, not merely affection, but the pure love of Christ. With this definition in mind, verse 8 becomes a powerful statement by Paul: "But whether there be prophecies, they shall fail; whether there be tongues, they shall cease; whether there be knowledge, it shall vanish away…but charity never faileth." To me this means that even the gifts of the spirit, such as prophecies, tongues, and even knowledge, will pass away, but the "pure love of Christ" is enduring and lasting in all situations. Having the love for others that Christ would have is a key to being happy.

To find a greater level of spirituality, I began by setting goals to worship more often, read from the scriptures, pray consistently, attend church meetings, and serve in the congregation. I truly believe I became more spiritual and gained more confidence in my relationship with God. Yet, as I grew spiritually, I was surprised to experience pain rather than immediate happiness. My eyes were opened to see my imperfections with greater clarity—imperfections that I had lived with for many years came to the forefront and demanded that I address them. It was uncomfortable and painful to have my imperfections exposed. Perhaps this is why new converts have a hard time after the "spiritual high" of joining a church. Our lives are sometimes like a room with a single light bulb in the ceiling. The bulb illuminates the middle of the room, but shadows lurk in the corners. These corners are where we hide our imperfections. We suppose that if they are out of sight they are taken care of. Many of us have become experts at hiding our imperfections in the corner and protecting those corners from anyone's line of sight. We feel threatened if anyone gets too close to the corners to see what is hidden.

As we grow in spirituality, we invite a brighter light into our lives—a light so strong that the shadows disappear, and all of our imperfections come into plain view. At first it is hard to understand that this light is healing, and we resist it. As we start to see what has been hidden away for so many years, we experience pain in the form of humility, and we feel remorse and the need to repent. The ego tries to block the light so that the imperfections remain hidden. The ego will convince you, if you let it, that the pain you are feeling is someone's fault or that you can be a spiritual person without addressing the cobwebs and dust in the corners of your life. Many of us find this so painful that we then back away from the light and let the ego shadow the corners once again, becoming quite comfortable with our shadowed corners. I have learned that the process of shining a light into my darkened corners requires continual exercise. Like physical exercise, if we stop too soon, the pain is for naught, and our exercise is in vain. I challenge you to stick with it, work through the pain with God's help, and let his light shine brightly in your life.

When I was younger, we always did spring cleaning. It was a dreadful time when we opened up the house to air it out and clean it from top to bottom. My job was washing the walls. I was surprised at how dirty the walls had become in just one year. In fact, that wasn't the only surprise. Every year I would argue that the walls looked fine and didn't need cleaning. It wasn't until my stepmother took a wet cloth and wiped a small portion of the walls to show just how dirty it was that I understood. It is that way with us as well; we don't realize the "dirt" in our lives until we wash a bit of it away and see the contrast. Sometimes it is just too much to deal with, and we learn to be satisfied with "dirty walls" and procrastinate our spiritual awakening. A spiritual awakening is an essential part of becoming happy. If we are not aware that the pain we experience by the new light in our life will lead us to greater ability to be happy, we may miss the opportunity and go back to start over again. I believe that there is a misconception among religious people that becoming spiritual automatically leads to happiness. Spirituality is an important element in being happy, and I suggest that an essential step is to acknowledge your divine nature, decide to reacquaint yourself with your maker, and, at the same time, decide that a God who loves you will not allow anything to happen in your life that is not for your benefit. It is not what happens to you that matters; it is how you deal with what happens to you that determines whether you achieve satisfaction and happiness.

At the same time, I know a lot of spiritual people whom I would not classify as happy or even satisfied with the life they are living. It is as if they alone are carrying the cross of Jesus on their backs as a statement of how to live a righteous life. Many suffer with dignity in the name of Jesus and believe it is the way Jesus wants them to live their lives. However, in Philippians 4:11, Paul says, "For I have learned, in whatsoever state I am, therewith to be content." Paul learned that whatever state he is in, good or bad, rich or poor, he can be content. You too can learn this.

There are also people who retreat to a life based on a religious checklist, thinking that once they check the box on repentance, charity, hope, forgiveness, getting married, having children, and attending church regularly, they will find happiness. There is no checklist of things that you can do to be happy. It is not about doing things as much as it is about "becoming." Being happy is not a destination; it is the way.

I urge you to get to know your maker. Just as an acorn is an oak having the blueprint of a great tree inside of it, your divine nature is God-like, and if you start to cultivate your divine nature and use it as a blueprint for how to live your life, it will empower you to be happy.

Practice empowering yourself and others to be happy

Being happy is not sitting back and letting God do all the work. You are still the driver, but now God is at the wheel. Let him guide you and be directed in all your situations and circumstances. The point here is to do something.

- Consider a time when you felt very happy or very peaceful. Be still, and let that feeling fill your body. This feeling has power. Now extend that feeling to the people around you. Do it right now. You will experience greater peace and happiness. You can do this anytime you want to feel peace.

- Clear your conscience so you can better align with your divine nature.

- If you are in a situation where you feel you are pleasing someone to make them happy, serve them with love instead.

- Be the miracle in someone's life.

Points to remember

- Consider yourself a partner with God in all things.

- Love and happiness have power and energy. As you become happy, you will empower those around you. Let your happiness flow outside of you and touch those around you.

- Ask God to help you see those around you with love, not as people you need to please to make happy.

- Share this book with those who you feel you need to support emotionally. Empower them take responsibility for their own happiness.

- Be a Good Samaritan by giving adequate service. You will know when it is adequate by the feelings of peace and happiness in serving.

- Allow light to shine into the corners of your life. It may be uncomfortable, but with God as your partner, you can live a shadow-free life and be happy.

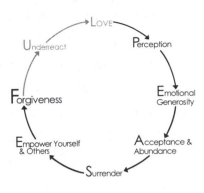

Chapter 7
Forgiveness

You cannot give away what you do not have. If you are not at peace with yourself, you cannot share peace with others. If you do not love yourself, the love you give to others will be minimized. If you do not forgive yourself, you will have a hard time forgiving others.

Learning how to forgive has been one of the greatest gifts I have ever received. Forgiving yourself and others will bring you greater peace than you can imagine. I have heard it said that forgiveness brings every gift that God has for you. It is truly one of the fundamental principles of the Happiness Factor. Do you need to forgive? Are there people that have caused you harm, hurt your feelings, or offended you? What starts as the smallest of incidents will turn into the greatest of rage if left unchecked. The ego will exaggerate the emotion and the incident, turning it into something bigger and more offensive that demands revenge. Ultimately, we either choose revenge or we choose to forgive.

Let's not kid ourselves, forgiving is hard, and the difficulty is not based on the magnitude of the offense. Sometimes the smallest of things are the hardest to forgive. I used to think that I was an expert at forgiving, that I didn't take offense and didn't hold grudges. Because I thought

I didn't need to forgive, I didn't pay attention to it. Forgiving isn't something that we are purposefully taught how to do. The process of forgiveness is typically taught in a religious setting and associated with repentance. I was taught that in order to forgive I had to confront the other person, air my grievance, and ask forgiveness. To me, that meant I had to become best friends with the person who offended me, making it doubly hard. Becoming friends with someone who has offended you or hurt your feelings is a very difficult thing to do. Not only is it scary, but sometimes we take offense to little things that are only made bigger by confronting the other person. I was once approached by a woman in my church congregation who asked me to forgive her for ill thoughts about me. I forgave her right there on the spot. Or so I thought. What should have been the end for me was just the beginning. I began to second guess what I could have done to make her think bad thoughts about me. Did I offend her in some way? Did I say something wrong? Did I offend one of her children? What was it? I couldn't get if off my mind. What should have been a "clearing of the air" just made it worse for me, and I felt that I now needed to ask for her forgiveness.

Why is forgiving so hard? Because the ego is fed by revenge and will fight to keep you from forgiving. I erroneously thought that I didn't hold a grudge against anyone. I considered myself easygoing and able to let go of offenses. If I could let go of my mother abandoning me when I was young, then I could let go of anything. Forgiveness is hard if we don't practice it, and like anything, if we don't practice, we get rusty. When we take offense, the ego relishes in it and holds on to it like a life preserver. Indeed, it is offense that gives life and breath to the ego. Through offense the ego is stimulated and becomes active, providing every excuse and reason why the other person should come crawling back to you and beg forgiveness. Even then the ego may hold on to the memory as some souvenir of having martyred yourself. Whatever it is that hurt you happened in the past and does not exist in the present. Marianne Williamson says, "At a certain point, we forgive because we decide to forgive. Healing occurs in the present, not in the past. We are not held back by the love we didn't receive in the past, but by the love we're not extending in the present."[31] There is not one of us who can't find something to hold a grudge about and then use it as an excuse to be unhappy and without peace.

The ego is a great collector. It collects grudges and offenses and holds them out on display for the whole world to see. An offense is like a juicy secret; when you have one, you can't wait to share it with others, and it grows in the telling. Once you forgive, you no longer have that excuse, and the ego will rebel. The ego loves excuses. At first forgiveness feels awkward and foreign, but with practice you can become a master. At the end of the day, it comes down to a decision. Either you decide to forgive, or you decide that you would rather rot with anger and stress. If you are serious about having peace in your life and living happily, then you must forgive. Without forgiveness, the peace and happiness you might feel will be fleeting and momentary. Make the decision to forgive; learn to forgive, and do it daily—or hourly—if needed.

Selective remembrance—forgetting offenses

To some degree, we all have selective memories, and it puzzles me to try to understand why sometimes I can't remember anything and other times I can't forget. We all have a highlight film we play in our mind of stupid things we have done or said that we just can't forget. For the longest time, I thought it was simply the way things were until I learned that I can purposely forget things that bring me pain or cause me to lose peace. You too can learn how to forget. I know someone who has a terrible memory. He has a hard time with names, dates, places, and faces and admits that he has a horrible memory. However, if you were to listen to him for very long, you would realize that he has an amazing memory for things that have hurt his feelings. He can tell you the date, time, place, and names of people who have hurt his feelings. It is amazing how accurate his memory is when associated with pain. It is as if pain has been imprinted on his mind like nothing else. Perhaps it is because he is so full of painful memories that he cannot remember other things. We all have painful memories, and these memories are signs that your mind is wounded and in need of healing. That healing comes through forgiveness, and forgiveness is enabled by forgetting.

Earlier in the book, I talked about the miracle of changing your mind, of going to God and asking for your mind to be healed when it is wounded by ill thoughts and perceptions. Forgiveness occurs as our mind is healed and we forget incidents that cause us pain. Our thoughts are the source of pain and emotion, not the other way around. What about when you are right and justified in finding fault and being offended? It often comes down to the question of whether you want to be right or whether you want to be happy. Regardless of who is right and who is wrong, if you are judging someone else, you are wrong. This was very hard for me to understand. I had thought I didn't hold a grudge, but what I was doing was collecting evidence on why I should not trust someone or interact with him or her. It provided an excuse for every negative thought I had about this person. I was playing a sophisticated game of self-justification. Forgiveness is being willing to forget about what happened in the past and releasing the emotions and expectations. When we are offended—when someone makes us angry, or turns us to hate—instead of looking at him as the enemy we can learn to look at him the way God does. We can look at him as a great teacher to us— someone put in our path to help us learn to be forgiving. He can be our greatest teacher. How easy it is to love someone who loves us back—to love someone when everything is going right. It's so easy that we seldom learn life lessons that are essential to being happy. When someone is offensive to us, it is because his ego is acting out, and he has forgotten who he is; he is listening to the ego instead of his divine nature. In that regard, it is not real. If we then see his divine nature as God sees it, even though the offensive person cannot see it, we can then forgive and let go of the offense. Our view of the other person actually changes to a more compassionate and loving view.

Forgiveness is a willingness to see someone's divine nature while at the same time having a desire to heal our wounded mind. How then, is it done? Before I give you the steps to forgiveness, let me tell you something that happened to me. As I have mentioned before, it wasn't that long ago I experienced a very dark and troubling period in my life. I am not sure how it happened, but over the period of a few months, I went from feeling rather positive about my life to feeling that I was failing at all that was important to me. It was a stark realization that no matter what measure of success I used I was still failing. My relationship with my wife was on a downward spiral, my children were withdrawing from me, and no matter what I did to emotionally reunite with them, it did not work. At the same time, my job was in jeopardy. I felt valueless. The more I tried to add value to those around me and to my job, the worse it became. I began to see everyone as the enemy and wondered why they couldn't see the value I was bringing to them. It affected everything around me, and I felt I had nowhere to turn for help, and so I turned on everyone who could help me. Where before I had found satisfaction, I now found despair thinking that failing in my own home meant I had failed in life and nothing I did could compensate for the failure I had become. My eyesight actually changed. I literally began to see things differently. Instead of seeing the good in people, I began to see the negative in them and hung on to it as a reason to hate and despise them. It didn't matter who it was; I felt that everyone was out to get me. My whole attitude about life, church, family, and career was negative. I was so negative that my wife withdrew from me in order to prevent being contaminated by my negativity. I could only see what I wanted to see, and what I saw was that she was rejecting me, causing me to resent her. For peace and happiness to return, I needed to see things differently. Just as you would get corrective lenses to see correctly, I needed emotional corrective lenses.

A dear friend of mine gave me great counsel. Like most lessons in life, this was something I already knew, but the circumstances were just right for me to listen. The adage "When the student is ready, the teacher will appear" was very true in this case. As I was lamenting all of my woes to him, particularly about my wife and my boss, he had the courage to say, "It is not another person's problems that are making your life miserable; it is you and your own thinking that is making you miserable. This is all about you, not about them." At first I was offended and didn't want to listen. He gave me the book *A Return to Love* by Marianne Williamson. This was the first step in my decision to be happy. I devoured the book, and the most immediate learning was that in order for me to find peace—in order for me to find satisfaction and a level of happiness—I needed to forgive. I am not sure what happened, and I cannot recount the exact words or thoughts I had, but I am grateful that for a short moment I was open to counsel and I realized that I had the power to let go, to see people differently, and to forgive. It was not about them; it was about me and my own thinking. So forgive I did, and it had amazing results. As the light of forgiveness began to shine upon me, the shadows began to disappear, and I discovered cobwebs and dust in the corners of my life that needed to be taken care of. It was as if a vast collection of offenses was discovered, and I needed to sweep them away. An immense burden lifted off my shoulders, clouds parted, and with new light I began to see things, people, and events differently. My eyesight was corrected, and I began to see the divine nature of others instead of who I thought they were. As I began to encounter my own divine nature, I was able to see and experience the divine nature of others. I was unburdened from years of holding on to offenses, grudges, and the mistakes of others. I literally felt lighter, not just because of the unburdening, but because I felt full of light. It brought me peace that I had never before felt in my life.

Don't be fooled into thinking that you have no one to forgive. We all need to forgive. A daily practice of forgiveness and a simple prayer to see the innocence of others instead of their guilt has brought me unbelievable peace and happiness. It has transformed my life and brought me peace to be happy. In actuality, since all offense happens in the past and only lives in our minds, forgiveness is really *forgetting* the lovelessness of another and deciding to entertain only loving thoughts about them. The same can happen for you. Forgive and live. Forgive and be happy.

Offenses happen in the past. Even if it just happened, it occurred in the past, and the offense is only given life as long as you remember it. In order to be free of the emotion and of the offense, you need to have your mind changed so you can forget the offense. The beauty is that as your mind is healed through forgetting, the pain you feel in your heart will disappear. Here is an interesting story. I was recently applying for a new position and the hiring manager was someone with whom I had a struggled with several years earlier. It was a horrible time for me, and I felt stung, embarrassed, and chastised by this person. I had promised myself that I would never work for her again no matter how important or how great the job might seem. Yet here I was years later applying for a position in her organization. Time had passed—it had been several years, in fact—yet I could still remember the pain and embarrassment she had caused me. The pain itself was gone, but the memory lingered and created doubt in my mind as to whether it would happen again. I decided that I would approach her and clear the air by asking about the past and if she felt I could be successful working for her. Here is what she said, "Kirk, I have short-term memory for things like that. I have learned that it does me no good to hang on to things that are painful. Goodness, it has been four years, and I hope that we both have matured and grown up. I can't even remember what it was about." Wow! Can you imagine someone actually forgetting about something bad that happened? If this was true, then she was on to something that I wanted to learn.

Since then I have found that I can ask God to help me forget, to take the memory away from me so that I can no longer even conjure up times when I have been hurt. When we are hurt, the offense only lives on in our memories, and God will not interfere with our thoughts without our permission. We simply need to give him permission to cause us to forget those things and the people who have hurt us and help us learn from the experience. I have used this repeatedly, and I can witness that it is a true principle. I have actually forgotten about offenses and cannot remember them, and at the same time, I know that I am growing and learning. God is a healer. When we are hurt by our memories—when an offense lives on in our mind—we are in need of healing. Approach God with your wounded mind, give it to him—literally surrender it to him—and he will heal you. You might consider this simple prayer: "God, I am hurt, and my mind is wounded, and it needs to be healed by forgetting the offense. I give thee permission to heal my mind so that I no longer remember the incident. Help me to see this person as you see him. Help me only consider his positive traits. Help me to see him as you see him." It works.

When my mother abandoned me, I was blessed with not being able to recall much of what happened before or after the day she left. This forgetfulness has been a great blessing to me. Every time I say that, people roll their eyes and say I am blocking the experience and the feelings.

I don't think I'm blocking; I truly believe I am blessed to forget. My brother, on the other hand, remembers too much, and it has affected him for years. Just recently was he able to become sober after thirty-five years. Much of the pain he was trying to drown out had to do with being abandoned. It may take saying that prayer over an over again like a mantra. I had to do that recently and it really works. I just cannot remember what I was upset about. What a great blessing it is to forget. Sometimes, when you feel pain and your mind is wounded, it needs to be healed and you need to forget. Don't confuse this with a pain-killer that masks the pain only to return once the medication has worn off. Forgetting does not mask the pain; it literally dissolves the pain because you no longer remember it.

"But what about really hard things?" you might ask. Say your husband has left you for another woman or you were abused as a child. My answer would be the same—you need to forgive in order to be at peace and be happy. You cannot change other people. After my father remarried, I did not get along with my stepmother. She and I clashed from the start, making us both miserable. I could not change my stepmother, and she had as much right to be who she was as I did. The only thing I could change is how I thought about it and how I remember it. It is a matter of putting faith in God to heal your mind. Peace is inside of us. Not in other people. If you are waiting for your wife to change before you are happy, you will be waiting a long time. If you expect your children to change so that you can be at peace, you will be waiting a long time. If I had waited for my mother to acknowledge me and come back, I would still be waiting. Peace and being happy is not about the circumstances but how we react to them. Don't let someone else's ego tempt you to follow your own ego. Following your divine nature allows you to rise above and take the higher road—the road of forgiveness, which brings peace and happiness.

But what about justice? What about people getting what they deserve? Rest assured, people will get what they deserve. It is the law of nature; it is the law of God. But it is not your law; it is God's law. Leave it to him. Do you deserve to lose peace over making sure that someone else gets the pain she deserves? Your peace is too precious to be spent that way. This does not mean that you walk away from crime or shed light on acts that should be handled by the authorities. It means you approach it from the perspective of wanting to help the other person get the help she needs to return to love instead of acting out of fear. Sometimes the best thing you can to do is to shed light on something that brings you pain. But if you do it out of spite, if you do it to get revenge, or if you do it because the ego needs to be fed, you are doing if for the wrong reasons. Too often we want to give someone feedback to hurt them back for hurting us. When we approach this from the perspective of shining light on something to heal it, and to heal ourselves, we can approach it from love and not from anger.

Partial blindness—living judgment free

For many years, I would have problems with at least one person. It was like a plague that followed me wherever I went. Regardless of whether it was at church, at work, or in my family, there always seemed to be at least one person who I wanted to avoid because of something he or she had said or done. I began to expect it so that when I had a new assignment at church or a new job I would start to look for the one person who would give me the hardest time. We all have people like this in our lives, and it seems like we can't ever be rid of them. I must have been real good at looking for that one person because I always found who I was looking for. It took me a long time to realize that the problem was not with that one person but with me. This is hard to admit, but just like almost anything, once you admit it you can deal with it and move on.

When I was a teenager, my stepmother criticized and scrutinized me. Like most teenagers, I just wanted to be me; I wanted to be accepted and loved. My grades were excellent, I worked full-time, I was not into drugs, I didn't drink, and I tried to be responsible. Why, then, was my stepmother so intent on scrutinizing me to the point where I felt hopeless? I could not turn to my father or my siblings. The criticizing and scrutiny made me feel like my entire world was collapsing and everyone was out to get me. I prayed. I prayed fervently for help. The help came in the form of a dream where a man came to me and said, "If she really knew who you were, then she wouldn't treat you that way." It was a miracle. The next morning I woke up with renewed confidence in myself that the way she treated me was because she didn't know me—that if she really knew me she wouldn't treat me that way. With that insight, I gained the ability to see her differently; I began to see her innocence instead of her guilt. This is a universal law. If people really knew who we were, that we are all children of God, they would not treat us badly. The reverse is also true. If we really know someone and see them as a child of God, then we are more likely to give him the benefit of the doubt and not hold grudges against him. How do we get to know someone? The answer may be simpler than you think because you already know them. It is the ego that convinces you to not see someone as God sees them. When you begin to see people in that light—when you start to consider someone's innocence instead of their guilt—their divine nature instead of seeing their ego-based actions—then you are able to release them from the offense and easily forgive them. When your thoughts of someone turn from judgment to compassion, then your divine nature takes over, and you can see a new light in them. This new light is one of innocence instead of guilt. It is a small and simple prayer to ask to see a person as God sees them: "God, please let me see this person through your eyes." As we accept the Savior in our lives, we are committing to be like him and to see people the way he sees them and to think as he thinks. At the same time, we actually start to see ourselves as God sees us, and that gives us the power and confidence to act from a position of love instead of a position of fear.

Another aspect of this is to realize that our perception and judgment is biased. Being human, being imperfect, we are unable to have perfect judgment or to perceive things accurately. Not long ago, I read a paper that exposed the inaccuracy of eyewitnesses.[32] Eyewitnesses are unreliable because no one is a truly unbiased observer. We are simply incapable of it. When I pass judgment on someone, I am saying that I am right and they are wrong. But in reality, when I finally accept the truth that I am a biased observer and that I am not in a position to judge anyone, life becomes more peaceful. When I start to feel offense, I ask myself, "Who am I to judge? Maybe in their situation and from their perspective I would say and do the same thing." I cannot tell you how much peace it has brought me by to let go of things that would normally upset me. Now it just doesn't matter. How did this happen? Because I am trying to see people in their innocence instead of their guilt. I am asking God to correct my vision and admit that I am a biased observer. My biases became very clear to me a few years ago. I was attending a seminar at Harvard Law School on handling difficult conversations along with six hundred very intelligent, senior-level people. For one of the exercises, we were asked to watch a short video of two teams exchanging basket-balls in a gymnasium. Our task was to count the number of exchanges between the team wearing white jerseys. The lights were dimmed, and we all watched the thirty-second video. The instructor then asked the audience how many times the basketball was thrown between the play-ers with white jerseys. The answers varied greatly. I began to wonder if these smart people just could not count. How could one person count ten and another count fifteen or even twenty? After the instructor exhausted the possibilities, he asked if anyone saw anything else in the video worth noting. Only one person raised her hand. She asked, "Who was that guy in the gorilla suit?" What an absurd question! What was she talking about? A guy in a gorilla suit? The instructor asked the rest of us if we had seen a guy in a gorilla suit. Two people raised their hands. It was preposterous. I had watched the video, I was very attentive, and I consider myself to be a good observer. There was immediate buzz in the audience as everyone else was thinking what I was thinking. This couldn't be right. The instructor suggested, "Rather than debating it, let's just show the video again." Guess what? Right in the middle of the video—right in front of the white team—a guy in a gorilla suit walked across the floor! I didn't see it the first time—my mind didn't even register it! In my mind, it was a nonevent, and I would have argued about it until I was blue in the face defending what I saw. Our mind only sees what we want to see; we are biased! When I finally admitted that I am biased, that it is impossible see things correctly 100 percent of the time, I was released from the burden of being right. I can now say "I don't know" with greater confidence, and I can also look at a situation and *know* that I can't grasp all of the circumstances, and therefore I cannot judge. One thing that has helped me is to realize that we judge others by their actions and behaviors while we judge ourselves by our intent. As we learn that we are biased judges, we also begin to see beyond our own vision and into the intent of others.

Not that long ago, I was talking to a friend about my daughter. I went on and on about how great she is and my friend said, "You just think she's perfect." My response surprised me when I said, "No, I know that she is not perfect; I just choose to not see her imperfections." So often we are obsessed with someone else's imperfections that it is all we see. Seeing someone differently is a choice. In fact, the more I notice people's imperfections, the more of them I find and I know they can feel it themselves. Notice how you talk to a really good friend compared to someone you really don't care for. Don't you think they notice? They do. With my daughter, I choose to have partial blindness to only see her admirable traits. I didn't realize what power that had until I said it out loud, realizing that if I can be partially blind with my daughter then I can do it with anyone. As a test, I began to pray for partial blindness for those around me. It is a very powerful yet simple prayer to ask, "Dear God, I intend to only consider Jane's positive traits. Please bless me to be blind to the rest." I promise that as you say this prayer—and you may have to say it over and over again—you will find that you become blind to the imperfections of others. It is a wonderful and miraculous feeling when you look at someone as if he or she were your best friend. Partial blindness should not be a new concept to you. Anyone who has fallen in love has experienced this. It is captured in the familiar phrase, "love is blind," and it is so true. As you change your mind to see another's innocence—to extend compassion and emotional generosity to that person—you begin to see them as God sees them. When you do this, you are extending love, and that love can bring you peace because it partially blinds you to the faults of those around you. The beautiful part is that those around you will respond in kind, and you will find a greater rapport, a more productive relationship, and greater happiness. Just simply choose to see someone's positive traits instead of their imperfections, and it will bring you peace.

From contempt to compassion

When I started to pay better attention to my thoughts and my actions, I found that I was full of contempt for others. I was judging people based on what they wore, how they ate, how they talked, and how they reacted to me. I remember when I was having chemotherapy I would get so angry at people who smoked, drank, and harmed their bodies. I had done none of that, and yet I was the one with cancer. That was contempt. As a young man, I made fun of overweight people, I would condemn people with different religious or political views, and it went so far as to jokingly be offended when someone rooted for a basketball team other than the Chicago Bulls. I was living a contemptuous life, and it was not peaceful. It was not loving. I was not happy.

The transformation from contempt to compassion starts with a serious and simple acceptance that you are nobody to judge. I am not any more important than anyone else, and therefore, I cannot truly put myself in anyone else's shoes, and I cannot judge them. When we judge another, we are actually judging ourselves. I am now willing to consider that when someone yells at me or treats me unkind it is because they are acting out of fear and not love. They have forgotten who they really are and are listening to the ego. They have become blind to their own divine nature. If I let the ego take over then I too will react with fear and will hold it against them. The Bible says, "Vengeance is mine, sayeth the Lord." (Rom. 12:19) This means that vengeance is not ours —it belongs to God; when we hold on to it for ourselves, we are taking something that does not belong to us. It is one of those "hot potatoes" that does more harm to us than anyone else. Give to God what is his.

It has taken me a long time to understand that there is no such thing as justifiable anger. When you judge, when you attack, you are wrong even though you may be right. When we judge or condemn another, we are actually prescribing emotional punishment for ourselves. When you desire peace and happiness more than you desire to be right, you will let it go and you will see it's not worth it. You will begin to see people who hurt you as people who have lost their way—people who have forgotten who they really are and have lost touch with their divine natures. Let go of judgment. Realize that you are unable to judge—that there is no such thing as righteous judgment—and leave that to God. Surrender it to God, and you will find that you have been spending a lot of time and energy worrying about getting even with others. Energy you can now spend on loving kindness. There is no such thing as "getting even." Getting even means you have lost.

Forgiving family

It is a truism that the ones you care for the most can hurt you the most. We reserve our strongest and most difficult emotions for those who are closest to us, expecting them to be the most trusting and understanding. Most often that is someone in our family. During the dark period of my life I described earlier, I began to notice that friendships were more enduring and more endearing than family. As I listen to people, I notice how they talk about their relationships and the difference in how they speak about their family in contrast to their friends. I observed that the fashion of the day is to put your family down and claim their dysfunction as a right of passage. My informal research revealed that people are more understanding and forgiving of their friends than of their own family. I would hear, "My dad did this," or "My mother did this to me," or "My bother is a loser." It became clear to me that that family is held to a much higher standard than friends. This causes pain and a lack of peace. It was rare for me to find people who were at peace with their family. For most of my life, I considered myself "a man without a mother" and relished in all of the benefits that came with that moniker. These benefits included not having to buy and send a Mother's Day card and not feeling obligated to call or write. I liked not having to worry about pleasing her or living up to her expectations, because there were none. As I would listen to colleagues and friends talk about their mothers, I considered myself lucky to not have to hassle with all of that.

I was blessed to never once consider that her decision to leave made me less of a person. There is no way I could even imagine how hard the decision would be for a mother to leave three children and start a whole new life. But her decision was hers, not mine, and so much good came from it. I consider myself a very independent person; I am able to take care of myself, and I work hard. I like who I am, and part of who I am is because my mother left me. If I choose to use it, the fact that my mother left me would be the best excuse in the world for anything I wanted to do. But it would not bring me peace. I found peace in forgiveness.

We all have dysfunction in our families, and we all have issues with relatives in dealing with obligations, expectations, and past histories. When it comes to family, it is time to let the past stay in the past. If you are holding on to memories of what your mother did or what your father said at your high school graduation, or if your dad didn't show up to the big game because he was working, you are giving that singular event enormous power to rob you of peace and happiness. The event itself only lives on in your memory, and it only has the power that you give it. You can dissolve that power by forgetting about the event, learning from it, and moving on through forgiveness. Forgiveness applies to all categories of people: people you are fond of, people who are beloved to you, people you feel neutral about, and people you are in conflict with. All of these people are your enemies. These are the people that God said to pray for when he said, "Pray for your enemies and those who despitefully use you." The prayer you can offer is one of forgiveness.

Forgive yourself

You cannot give away what you do not have. If you are not at peace with yourself, you cannot share peace with others. If you do not love yourself, the love you give to others will be minimized. If you do not forgive yourself, you will have a hard time forgiving others. Everything we do to others, everything we say about others, and everything we think about others, we are really saying about ourselves. This is a very hard concept to grasp because we have never been trained to see it that way. As we work on ourselves, we become better equipped to add value to those around us.

Movies and television have made a cliché out of "finding yourself" by portraying that to find yourself you must get lost. Popular opinion is that in order to find yourself you need to escape to a faraway place where you magically find out who you are and then return a changed person ready to face what you left behind. When you merely change your surroundings without making a deliberate attempt to change yourself, you have only accomplished one thing: you have transported all of your problems to a new location. You don't have to escape to find yourself. You can find yourself right where you are, and it starts by taking a long objective look at who you are. You are a child of God. God is perfect, and he would not do anything or allow anything to happen that is not a pure expression of his love for you. You need to find the love God has for you, and you can do this by learning to love yourself. Forgiveness is a true expression of God's love. When we forgive another, we are acting as God would act, and we are expressing his love for them. That same expression of love occurs when you forgive yourself. Everything I have written about in this book not only applies to others but applies to you as well. You can ask God for the miracle of seeing yourself as God sees you. You can ask God to change your mind so you learn from your past mistakes but no longer remember them or condemn yourself for them. We have all done things that we wish we could undo. A harsh word or an angry response cannot be retracted once it is said. We cannot swallow our words once they are out. How do we handle that? What about really tough things? What about real sorrow and pain we have caused? How can we even dream of being happy when others we have hurt are not? You may even think that because of the things you have done you should never be happy; you may think that happiness is for people who don't have the sins and guilt that you have; you may think that you do not deserve to be forgiven and that you don't deserve to be happy. This is the ego talking, and you are not paying attention to your divine nature.

The fact is that everyone deserves to be happy, including you and the people you have hurt. God loves everyone the same; he wants the same for all of his children—including you! Remember that God's love is meant for everyone. This can sometimes be difficult to acknowledge because it contradicts the ego. It is the ego that convinces you that you cannot be forgiven because of all the wrong you have done and that you cannot be happy. It is the ego that hangs on to the memories of all your misdeeds, causing you misery and torment as you relive them. The atonement is not just for sinners. The atonement applies to our inadequacies and our faults and can compensate for the pain others' experience from our misdeeds and mistakes. To accept the atonement is to accept by faith that those we have injured will be comforted and healed by God if *they* allow it. Your obligation is to be *willing* to do all you can to make up for your misdeeds. You also need to admit that you may not know all that you can or should do, and you need to be willing to let God teach you what you can do to make up for past mistakes. Surrender this to God, and ask him to reveal to you what it is that you can do. Once you have done your part to seek forgiveness, it is not your responsibility to make someone happy—that is left up to the other person. Ask God to take the memory of your mistakes away from you and leave you with valuable lessons to help you grow and mature.

Practice forgiving by forgiving yourself

Have you ever looked at yourself? That seems like a funny question, doesn't it? How many times do we stand in front of a mirror each day and not really look at ourselves? There are days when I shave, brush my teeth, and comb my hair (what little there is of it)—all in front of a mirror—but I don't really see myself; I don't really look at who I am. It is time you take a look at who you really are. Go into the bathroom or sit in front of a mirror where your can clearly see your face, and take a long intense look at yourself. Look at your hair, your ears, your eyebrows, your eyelashes, and the color of your eyes. Look at yourself as if you want to memorize every minute detail of your face. Don't dwell on any one thing, like a wrinkle or a blemish, just look at yourself in detail. Take your time, and really study your face. Keep doing this until you feel uncomfortable. Then look into your eyes. Look through the front of your eyes and try and see your own soul. This is the place where you can speak to your innermost self. Concentrate on making contact with your inner self and divine nature. Now it is time to talk, to teach, to learn, and to forgive. From Marianne Williamson's book *A Return to Love*, I learned a prayer of self-forgiveness that I continue to use with a few modifications. Here is what I say to myself, and I share it with you as an example of what you can say.

> God loves all of his children.
>
> I am one of his children, and so God loves me.
>
> God is perfect, and he has made me perfectly.
>
> I have done some things that are wrong.
>
> I have done some things I am embarrassed about.
>
> I have made mistakes.
>
> I must have chosen wrongly, because I am not at peace.
>
> If I had to do them over again, I would do things differently.
>
> I want to be at peace.

Had I known better, I would have done better.

Had I known it would hurt others, I would have chosen differently.

I want to learn from my mistakes and only remember them so I can learn.

I forgive myself, and I release myself.

I forgive myself, and I release myself.

I forgive myself, and I release myself.

Continue to look at yourself in the mirror for a while, and let this sink in. Throughout the rest of the day, and maybe the next several days, keep saying to yourself, "I forgive myself, and I release myself." The releasing is to let go of any expectations you have regarding your mistakes, your past, and the pain you have caused. Releasing yourself is a way of letting go of the pain, the memory, and the thoughts.

Now you can start to forgive others. Forgiveness is like anything else—it takes practice. Make a practice of it by forgiving and releasing those who have hurt you, those who have caused you pain, or have caused you conflict. I am sure that, as you are reading this, someone has come to your mind that you need to forgive, and you recognize that you are not at peace with this person. This is the best indicator of the need to forgive. As you become sensitive to your level of peace with others, it will be a clear signal of when you must forgive in order to come back into peace. It doesn't matter who you start with, just pick the first person who comes to mind. Let's assume this person's name is David. Simply say out loud to yourself, "David, I forgive you and release you and wish you peace. David, I forgive you and release you and wish you peace. David, I forgive you and release you and wish you peace. David, I forgive you and release you and wish you peace. David, I forgive you and release you and wish you peace." Keep this short prayer in your mind all day long, saying it over and over again. You will know when you no longer need to forgive David when you start to feel at peace. Then pick someone else and do the same. As I did this, the most amazing thing happened to me. I became very aware of people who I did not feel at peace with. There were some people who I felt real pain when I thought of them and others where the pain was less severe. As I started to forgive them by using this short prayer of forgiveness, I felt free. I felt a real physical burden lifted off my shoulders and I became happy. This can happen to you. I say this small prayer all the time. There are always instances when I need to bring peace back into a situation by using this prayer. Whether it be a rude grocery clerk, a coworker, my children, or my extended family that causes me to lose peace, this prayer allows me to release any feelings about it and forget about it without feeding the ego. The ego is useful in this case because, if you pay attention to the ego, you will know when you need to forgive. When ever your reaction to a person or a situation includes the words "stupid," "jerk," or "idiot"—whenever you get mad at something someone has said or done, regardless of who they are, it is a sign that you are out of peace. To restore peace you must forgive.

I promise that as you start to pay attention to when and how you use those words you will find that forgiveness can restore your peace and allow you to be happy. Forgiveness is a miracle you can bring into your life; it is something that you are in full control of. You don't need to ask permission, and you don't need to wait for anything. This is something you can do right now. Those you forgive will know you have forgiven them without you having to say a word to them. If you need to tell them, you will be inspired at the right moment and place to share it with them, and it will be a miraculous event. It is more important to forgive than it is to wait for the right time to forgive.

This past summer I visited my mother. This would be the fifth time I had seen her from the time I was eight years old. Over the forty years since she abandoned me, I felt that I had forgiven her, but I hadn't really gone through the process of forgiveness. Using the small prayer above, I forgave her and released all the feelings I had about it. There was an amazing release of emotion, and I had a desire to visit her. I had a longing inside to reconnect with her and perhaps have a relationship with her. When I visited her, I wasn't sure if or when the right moment would be to express my forgiveness, but it came and it was a wonderful moment.

The only thing keeping you from these wonderful moments is your own fear of forgiveness. Holding back forgiveness is sometimes used as a subconscious means of waiting for "payback." Holding out for someone to pay for his or her mistakes. Forgiveness is not a concession that someone else is right and you are wrong, because it really doesn't matter who is right. It is a choice you make to prioritize being happy over being right and choosing peace regardless of the circumstances. As you practice forgiveness you will realize that it becomes easier the more you do it. Don't waste another minute being miserable. It is time to forgive, it is time to release all the emotions and expectations you have of those you need to forgive. When you begin this process, you are one step closer to being happy.

Forgiveness has side benefits that scientists are just now realizing. In 1985 there were only five completed studies on the subject of forgiveness. Since then hundreds of studies have been conducted all over the world. ABC News reported on January 2, 1998 that "studies show that letting go of anger and resentment can reduce the severity of heart disease and, in some cases, even prolong the lives of cancer patients." The University of Montgomery administered a study in 1995 that "analyzed how much the desire for revenge (i.e., the opposite of forgiveness) factors into the committing of a crime. The study clearly indicates that forgiveness education could play a key role in reducing the vengeful responses that lead to criminal acts." There are "many family therapists successfully using forgiveness as a tool to reconcile couples when other techniques have proved ineffective."[33]

When we can realize and admit that we have all been hurt and that we are in need of healing, then we can seek the help we need. The ego is subversive and capable of being suspicious of everything and anything. You must make a conscious decision to focus on the positive and let the rest go. In fact, the decision you need to make is even more fundamental: do you want to hold a grudge or do you want to be happy?

Practicing forgiveness

- Forgiveness will be liberating especially if you practice it regularly and consistently. Look for the signs that give you a warning that you need to forgive. These signs include negative feelings toward yourself or someone else, as well as avoidance of another person and anger. These are all indicators that you need to forgive.

- I suggest you ask God to open your mind to all the people you need to forgive, and you will find there are more than just a few. Forgive them. Don't think twice about it. Forgive them, and you will be happy.

- Who is the person you avoid seeing or talking to? Picture that person in your mind and now say, "I forgive you, and I release you." It may take a several times repeating that before the burden you feel is lifted off your shoulders. Persevere, it will happen.

- Now think of someone that you know doesn't like you—someone you would consider an enemy—and forgive them as well.

- In every encounter, instead of judging someone, silently say, "I bless you." Or "May God bless you." You then move from contempt to compassion and compassion leads to happiness.

- Think of the thing you have done that you regret the most. That is an indicator that you need to forgive yourself. Follow the simple prayer of self-forgiveness to truly and completely forgive yourself.

Points to remember

- Thoughts precede our feelings and emotions. Forgetting the incident heals our minds of the painful thoughts, dissolving the pain we feel regarding the event.

- Our judgment is biased. We never see anything as it is; we only see things based on our perception.

- Seek to be partially blinded to the faults and traits of those around you. There is no purpose or reason to see the faults of another. You will literally begin to see the person differently.

- Remember, you cannot give what you do not have. Forgive yourself. God will guide you to do what you can to make up for mistakes and offenses.

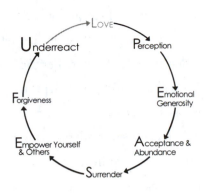

Chapter 8
Underreact

Expect the best, accept the rest, and mildly neglect.

One of the greatest secrets to being happy is found in this short but powerful sentence: "I choose to underreact." This short sentence, whether vocalized or said silently, holds one of the greatest of all powers—the power to manage your response to any given situation. This powerful statement has brought me peace and happiness, reducing my stress level and allowing me to live a worry-free life. Can you imagine being worry free? Can you imagine living stress free? The principle of underreacting can not only reduce stress and worry but eliminate them from your life.

Everywhere I go, I observe people overreacting. I overheard Bill tell his friend how he literally went "ballistic" when he learned his teenage son had been caught shoplifting. Kendra was on her cell phone in the Denver airport and lashed out at her mother for not remembering her birthday. Eric commented to a coworker how he yelled and screamed at his daughter for being two hours late on her curfew. After a merger, Jason might lose his job. He has to decide to take an outside offer or stay through the merger and doesn't have enough information to help him make the choice he has to make. Jennifer lost her car keys and was yelling at her kids to get out of the car and help her look for them. A mother in the grocery store just left her cart in the middle of the aisle and left the store because her toddler was acting up. Choosing to under-react will put things in perspective and create constructive and positive feelings instead of negative ones.

Sure, you say, underreacting is a cop-out because sometimes things happen that require a serious response. Don't confuse underreacting with a lack of seriousness. Think of underreacting as the antidote to overreaction. Too often an overreaction is an ego-based reaction that ultimately keeps you from finding the truth and prevents you from find-ing the best resolution to a problem. When I have overreacted, I too often have been blinded by emotion and other feelings to make good decisions. Overreacting prevents me from taking the time to listen and learn. Overreacting is fed by the ego. Also, don't confuse underreacting with apathy. Underreacting doesn't mean you don't care or are uncon-cerned; it means that you approach serious things with the sobriety they deserve and without the drama. Underreacting takes courage and con-centration. Underreacting keeps my head clear, and I am much more productive. The amazing benefit of underreacting is that I have a more appropriate response to all that happens around me.

There is another very important side to underreacting that needs to be considered. People who overreact are not told the truth and are sometimes purposefully not brought into a circle of confidence. We all know people who "freak out" over the littlest things. If you know this about someone, you try to protect them by not telling them things that will cause them to freak out. I consider myself a pretty good listener and a good counselor, but my children have sometimes not confided in me because they are afraid I will "freak out." I am sure there are things that any parent would freak out about, but there are some things that I wish I had not overreacted to. "Freaking out" can show mistrust and judgment when we want to show care and concern. Having "freaked out" in the past, my children think they are doing me a favor by keeping things from me when, in actuality, the opposite is true. If you think about the people you confide in—the people you trust the most—I can bet you that these are not people that freak out. "Freaking out" is also a signal to others that you are more concerned about your own reaction and feelings than you are about the person you are listening to. When you underreact, you keep a level head. You hear the truth more often, and you demonstrate interest in what the other person has to say by keeping the attention focused on the situation instead of your own reaction and emotions.

The power of the resurrection

For years and years, I have learned and taught the resurrection. What a beautiful doctrine that mankind can be reborn and reunited with the spirit to form a perfect body. Yet, it wasn't until recently that I learned to apply this doctrine and principle in my daily life. Let me explain. Having traveled all over the world visiting many churches and engaging in many religious discussions, I have noticed that many people fixate on the crucifixion of Jesus Christ. Don't get me wrong; I don't want to minimize this event in any way. I also want to express my appreciation for the suffering of the Savior to take upon himself the sins of the world. But to me, the crucifixion represents suffering, pain, and death. My observations are that some people believe that suffering brings them closer to God. That to suffer makes them Christ-like. In some ways this is contrary to the doctrine of the atonement where Jesus suffered for us so that we would not have to suffer; he took upon himself the infirmities of the world so that we do not have to suffer unnecessarily. Certainly there will be negative consequences to our actions that will bring some amount of suffering upon us. But no matter how big or small the sin, God has taken my suffering upon him so that I do not have to suffer alone. However, the crucifixion is meaningless without the resurrection. Death and suffering are meaningless without the hope of relief through a rebirth or resurrection. The Bible states "that he was buried, and that he arose again the third day according to the scriptures: For as in Adam all die, even so in Christ shall all be made alive." (1 Cor. 15:4-22) Death is inevitable, and by the power of the resurrection, we shall all be made alive.

You might be asking, "What does the resurrection have to do with everyday situations, and what does it have to do with being happy?" We can apply the principle and miracle of the resurrection in almost every situation. Consider the symbology of the crucifixion and resurrection for a moment. The crucifixion, or "death," can be defined as a separation from God. When we sin or when we align ourselves with the ego, we separate ourselves from our divine nature, thus separating ourselves from God. When we suffer or experience consequences of our poor judgment, we sometimes feel alone and separated from the very God who created us. Also, there may be times when we feel a symbolic separation when we are faced with a difficult decision or feel tremendous anxiety over an immediate crisis. The Bible tells us that, after three days, Christ rose again and was made "new" through the power of the resurrection. We can tap into that power by allowing the resurrection to empower our lives. When I am faced with a difficult decision, even one that needs immediate attention, I have found that by taking a symbolic "three days" to reflect, meditate, and contemplate, I can maintain peace and see the situation more clearly than I did before. There have been many cases when the issue has disappeared during that time and did not even require my response. The magical "three days" is underreacting and allowing God to work a miracle by either guiding you in the right direction or helping you make a decision. This has significance in my own life as I was faced with a serious decision to have major surgery. When diagnosed with a new form of cancer after seven years of being cancer free, my doctor recommended radical exploratory surgery to find the source to be followed by several rounds of chemotherapy. I felt unsure of the surgery and felt pressure from family and friends to have the surgery quickly. Instead, I took some time to let a miracle take place. During that time, I received a call from a friend who worked as a director at the American Cancer Society, suggesting that I talk to the head doctor of cancer research. The doctor who I was to call happened to be passing through and stepped into my friend's office while we were on the phone. After I described the dilemma, he told me to skip the surgery. This year I will be fourteen years cancer free without having to experience the painful surgery. Taking the magic and symbolic "three days" resulted in a miracle.

In reality, there are very few times when you absolutely have to make an immediate decision. Sure, there are many people around you—the car salesman, the telemarketer, your friends, and family—who insist you make a decision or "lose the deal of a lifetime." But really, there are so few things in this life that just can't wait. I promise you that by taking the magic "three days" before reacting or deciding, you will make much better decisions, and your stress level will decrease significantly and possibly be eliminated. I am not suggesting that you set a timer for seventy-two hours; rather, you should symbolically step back and ask for a miracle; ask to see things differently, to understand the truth. As you step back, you will find a great power to deal with the things that cause you anxiety and suffering. You will find a reuniting with your divine nature, enabling God to inspire and guide you.

Mild neglect

In a friend's office, he has a small plaque that reads, "Expect the best, accept the rest, and mildly neglect." The plaque faces outward to his visitors, not to himself. My friend, Ted Buckland, explains that his motto is a reminder of how to deal with everyone, including his children, his wife, his employees, and visitors. He wants everyone to know that he expects the best from them and that they can and should expect the best from him. He went on to explain that oftentimes we forget to expect the best from others, because it is so easy to expect people to fail. It is as if we watch very closely to find evidence that someone is failing. When you seek the best in someone—when you expect the best—you will most likely find it. Oftentimes we fool ourselves into thinking that we are looking for the best when deep inside we are anticipating failure.

"Accept the rest." Often, when we have high expectations, we are usually met with disappointment. Learning to accept the rest means learning to be satisfied with what *is*, with whatever the outcome happens to be. There are so many instances when we beat a dead horse by arguing over what could have been and nitpicking at the difference between what was expected and what was delivered. Accepting the rest is finding satisfaction with what *is*.

When it comes to learning to underreact, learning how to mildly neglect is key. Mild neglect is the opposite of nagging. Whether you call it nagging or offering gentle reminders, it is the same. In the end, it is all nagging. Nagging is destructive and creates stress for the person doing the nagging and distrust for the one being nagged. Mild neglect is a form of underreacting as you learn to let go of the outcome by neglecting it mildly. No one likes to be micromanaged. As a manager, I have guaranteed to my employees that I will not micromanage them, and I give them permission to call my attention to it if I ever do. There have been times, however, when I have nagged my children to death. I have found it so easy to find fault and to not be able to see beyond the chasm between my expectations and their performance. This is particularly frustrating when I see my child heading in the wrong direction. Almost immediately I want to correct his path. Too often I have stepped in when the greater lesson would have been for me to mildly neglect, allowing my child to learn to correct his own direction and complete the task on his own. Mildly neglecting means that we allow some of our expectations to go unmet by underreacting. It means allowing our children and others to be accountable for their own actions and suffer the natural consequences. Mild neglect does not mean total neglect or negligence. It simply means that you stop nagging and stop micro managing. Nagging only causes contention and, in the end, causes you to lose peace. Let it go.

Let me give you an example from my own home. Like any parent, we want our children to grow up to be responsible and polite. One of our sons has a hard time calling people back who leave messages for him. However, he had an aversion to calling anyone back, and we felt it was irresponsible. We constantly nagged him to return phone calls to his church leaders, teachers, and coaches. Finally, we realized we were taking ownership for things he should be doing. We didn't change our expectations, but we finally accepted all that he could do and chose to mildly neglect by not nagging and letting him take responsibility for his own messages and phone calls. Is he better at this? Not really. But we changed our approach and found greater peace in our relationship with him. The nagging would not have changed his behavior either. By not nagging him so much, we are able to gently motivate and encourage him rather than getting on his back for what he has not done. We all felt more peace and have a much better relationship. Expecting the best, accepting the rest, and mildly neglecting is underreacting in action and can bring peace and empower you to be happy.

No one is out to get you

Suppose a friend comes to you and, with all sincerity, says someone is out to get him. Suppose he told you he was being followed and wanted you to protect him. How would you respond? Sounds a bit dramatic, doesn't it? However, if you listen closely to the people with whom you interact, you will notice that many of them think someone is out to get them. It will sound something like, "My boss hates me. My ideas threaten him, and he doesn't listen to me." Or they might say, "My brother's new girlfriend is so jealous of me. She hates it when I hug him." The list goes on and on. The ego loves a conspiracy, and it's a way for the ego to trick you into thinking that you are so important that people will spend time thinking up ways to make your life miserable. I have done this—we have all done this—taking the smallest amount of evidence—a frown, a comment, a glance—and turning it into a full conspiracy against us. There may be people you know who are obsessed with this and create elaborate theories of why people are out to get them. It is easy for us to get caught up in this and feed the flames by agreeing with them. Don't we all love drama? Don't we all love juicy rumors and "dirt" about our family, coworkers, and friends? There are also those people who love to stir the pot. They like to create drama around them, and drama seems to follow them wherever they go. Just like an intense scene in a soap opera or a movie, drama in our lives creates anxiety and stress. Anxiety and stress, in turn, contaminate our attempts to live peacefully and can be speed bumps on the road to being happy. What a shame.

When it comes to conspiracy theories and soap operas, I choose not to participate. I choose to underreact. I simply wait until there is more evidence to support one theory or another and then have compassion for those involved. The same is true with all the drama you tend to attract. By choosing to underreact, you can do away with the drama that creates anxiety and stress and thus live more peacefully and happily. Drama attracts drama. Distrust attracts distrust. Underreacting attracts peace, tranquility, and demonstrates a life of integrity.

True emotions

Recently, I overheard a mother punishing a young boy for hitting his sister. "Why did you hit her?" she asked. "Why did you do that?" It made me remember the myriad of times my own parents asked me why I teased my sisters or why I did this thing wrong or that thing wrong. I was bewildered because there was no answer. How many of us really know why we react a certain way or feel certain things? If you were to study the range of experiences of people who are generally satisfied with life and compare it to those who are unhappy, you would find little difference. We all have approximately the same disappointments and setbacks—the same amount of wins and losses. The difference is not the circumstances or the situations; it is in how we react to what happens to us. One of the most interesting factors in learning to be happy is learning to identify emotions and the associated thought patterns so as to make the necessary adjustments. In a 1997 study, Narella Ramanaiah and Fred Detwiler found that the better people are at identifying the source of their feelings, the more apt they are to overcome life's disappointments.[34] I don't know about you, but this is revealing to me because there are times when I am feeling angry, sad, or anxious but unable to pinpoint exactly what happened to make me feel that way. Without being able to understand the source of my feelings, I am reacting from a set of responses I have learned rather than from my true emotions and feelings. An important aspect of living a happy life is learning how to identify what you are feeling. Have you ever been angry without knowing why? Have you ever been sad or depressed and not really known why? Many times I feel negativity, and I don't know why. A few days ago, I came home from work in a bad mood. In the past, it would have escalated to a fight or some other outburst of anger. Fortunately, I recognized I was on edge and went into my office to meditate and try to identify what had happened to cause me to lose peace. As I was meditating, I recalled a meeting with my supervisor that did not go as well as I had planned. It was a positive meeting but didn't meet my expectations. Once the event was identified, I could adjust my thoughts to handle the disappointment that occurred earlier in the day. In this case, I surrendered my feelings to God, knowing that the event occurred in the past, and asked him to help me learn from it and to remember only the positive aspects of the meeting. Thankfully, I was able to identify it and handle it before my emotions were transmitted in the form of anger toward my wife or children. I had carried that disappointment with me all day and had lost peace over it. Learning to identify the source of your feelings will help you to react appropriately. Choosing to underreact gives you the time to identify those emotions and feelings. One way to do this is to realize that a negative thought or feelings of disappointment or anger are just that. They are thoughts, feelings, and emotions. They do not define who you are. A negative thought does not mean you are depressed. It is just a negative thought.

I choose to underreact so that I can: (1) recognize that I am feeling angry, and (2) understand the source of my anger so that I am better able to deal with and manage my emotions rather then letting them flow over into other areas. People who are able to identify the source of their emotions and feelings are more capable of formulating a more appropriate response rather than just reacting to the situation.

Quite recently I also recognized that anger was my first and most common response to any negative situation. The good news was that I was consistent. The bad news was that it hurt everyone around me when I was the one hurting the most. It was a miracle to realize that I could choose a different response than anger. I could choose to underreact instead.

This simple yet powerful choice has taught me that anger is the outward demonstration of other internal emotions based in fear—fear of not being in control, fear of not being loved, fear of not being valued, fear of not being right, fear of not being trusted. The list went on and on. I was not so much an angry person as I was a fearful person. Rather than turning my emotions outward in anger, I needed to first understand the source of my feelings. I started asking myself, "What are you afraid of?" and after a few times, I learned that I had so little to be afraid of that anger was actually a defense mechanism for fear. It kept me from addressing my fears. Choosing to underreact has helped me to learn and understand the source of these feelings and deal with them in a more positive way. This is one aspect of emotional intelligence as described by Dr. Daniel Goleman in his book *Emotional Intelligence*.[35] Learning to identify the source of your emotions and learning to articulate how you feel is an important aspect of learning to be happy.

Underreacting can be taught. My daughter helped me learn this concept during a recent visit. Her five-year-old son was quite angry about not being able to "transform" a newly acquired Transformer toy. Let me share with you the dialog between my daughter and her son Markie:

"Markie," she said, "what is it you are feeling?"

Markie said, "That Transformer is stupid; I can't do it."

Meghan reached out to him, touched him on the shoulder gently, and said, "I want to know what you are feeling, can you tell me that? Can you tell me what you feel?"

Markie yelled, "The Transformer is stupid."

"Well," she said, "the Transformer is just a toy; it can't be smart or stupid. Are you frustrated?"

"I can't transform it. It's stupid."

"Markie, it sounds like you are frustrated and could use some help. Would you like some help? Are you frustrated? Tell me how you feel."

The conversation continued for a few minutes until she had coaxed out of him that he was frustrated and exasperated with trying to transform the Transformer without success. I understood completely because

I had tried to do it and couldn't either, so I concluded that the toy was stupid as well. This small interaction between my daughter and my grandson taught me a valuable lesson: we can be taught to identify our feelings. When we are caught up in the moment, it is very difficult to step back and take the time to identify what we are feeling and why. Choosing to underreact will give you the time you need to do so. My daughter was being a coach to my grandson. Wouldn't it be great to have a coach with us all day long to help us avoid overreacting, to help us identify the source of our emotions and feelings? You can imagine how impressed I was with my daughter…until she told Markie, "Take the Transformer to Grandpa. I am sure he can help you do it!"

Mind the gap

If you have ever been to London, you know the phrase, "Mind the gap." The phrase itself has become a mantra of pop culture. "Mind the gap" is a warning to watch your step as you board or disembark from the underground trains so you don't step into the gap between the platform and the train. While in most stations the gap is narrow and manageable, in some stations the gap is quite large. This is particularly concerning during rush hour when you are literally pushed on and off of the trains by the crowds. "Mind the gap" is announced by the train conductor at almost every stop and has become so popular you can buy t-shirts and stickers with the phrase. While minding the gap at the underground station is important for your safety, there is a more significant gap that, when minded, will enable you to be happy. It is the gap between stimulus and response.

The idea that there is a gap between any stimulus and our response holds significant meaning to Steven Covey. He relates that during a sabbatical with his family in Oahu, Hawaii, he was wandering the book stacks in the college library one day and noticed a book that caught his interest. As he looked through the book, his eyes fell on a paragraph that powerfully influenced the rest of his life. Covey says, "The paragraph communicated the simple idea that there is a space between any stimulus and the response to it. The key to our growth and happiness is how we use that space. The idea hit me with fresh, unbelievable force. It was like an inward revolution."[36] In his book, *7 Habits of Highly Effective People*, Covey describes the gap that needs to be minded.[37] Consider that anything that causes an emotional or physical response from you is a stimulus and that there is a gap between that stimulus and your response. You own that gap; it is yours. We have been given instinctual responses such as fright or flight in times of danger for protection. You put your hand on a stove and without thinking, you retract it. The response to quickly withdraw your hand is an instinctual response to protect you from further harm. We can actually choose how we respond to the stimuli around us. There are times when our personal safety depends on how fast we respond. If the car in front of you were to slam on the brakes, your ability to respond quickly and appropriately could avoid a serious accident. Just as we have learned to adjust our speed when we see the brake lights of the car ahead of us, we have learned responses to other stimuli in our life that are now automatic. When we feel threatened, criticized, put down, embarrassed, or we simply don't get our way, we respond the way we have learned to respond. Though we might not think so, our emotional responses are by choice. When we are given a compliment or someone does something kind for us, we also respond the way we have learned to respond. These learned responses become automatic and immediate unless we recognize that we can control our response—that we can control the gap between the stimulus and our response. Every response is by choice. Your anger, stress, depression, and sadness are all responses to some stimulus in your life. Just as you can choose to be happy, you can choose to be sad, angry, or afraid. The gap I am talking about is real. It is powerful. How you mind the gap can have a dramatic effect on being happy. Choosing to underreact gives you the power to take control of the gap and use it to your advantage.

We all know someone who overreacts and immediately thinks of the worst-case scenario. Overreacting is a trained response, and with conscious effort, these trained responses can be unlearned, and a new response can replace them. When you are confronted with a stimulus that has the potential to worry you, to cause you stress, anger or depression; simply say to yourself, "I choose to underreact. I choose peace over this." Then take the symbolic "three days" to choose an appropriate response. My experience has been that as I underreact, many of the problems I face disappear. Recognizing that most things that happen to me do not need an immediate response has allowed me to manage the gap more effectively, and as a result, I have much more peace.

Practicing to underreact

- Take a breath. The next time you are faced with a dilemma or you feel yourself overreacting, take a breath. Let that be a signal to you that you need to underreact.

- Take a step backward. I mean literally step away from a situation. If you are being pressured by a salesman, by your son or daughter to make a decision, if you are feeling compelled to react, simply step backward and say, "I choose to underreact." The physical step backward helps you withdraw momentarily and gives you the space you need to underreact.

Points to remember

- Recognize there is a gap between any stimulus and your response to it. You own that gap, and you can choose your response.

- Expect the best, accept the rest, and mildly neglect by allowing some of your expectations to go unmet.

- Take the magical and symbolic "three days" to contemplate and meditate on a decision or challenge that faces you. You will find that new answers and perspective come your way.

- Identify the source of your feelings and emotions during the "three days" mentioned above. Learn to step back and analyze your emotions and their source. As you do that, you become an observer of your actions rather than a participant. As an observer, you can choose your reaction—you can choose to underreact.

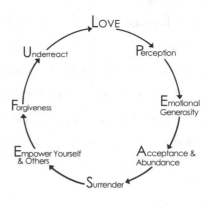

Chapter 9

Love

Love dissolves all negativity, discord, conflict, anger, contention, fear, and strife.

To begin this chapter on love, let me first go back to the chapter on surrender because the two concepts are so tightly connected. Let me explain. To love is to live a life of surrender. A life of surrender is a life free of worry, problems, and stress. Once again, I ask, can you imagine a worry-free life? If you can imagine it, you can live it. It is all through surrender—surrendering to God. God is love, and so when you surrender to God, you are surrendering to love. It is a daily practice for me to surrender and keep my mind turned to God and to choose love over all else. As I start my day I meditate to clear my mind, asking that God fill it with his will and his love. I surrender every encounter, every appointment, every task, and every situation to God, asking that love be my primary purpose and that I be able to recognize his hand in all things and see the miracles that happen on my behalf. I ask to be of service to those in need. As the day closes, I dedicate it to God and ask to learn from all that has happened, allowing me to love more and to be a better instrument the next day. I can't even begin to explain the blessings, the abundance of peace, and the happiness that has come into my life as a result of making love the highest priority over all else. Relationships have been healed, resentment has faded, miracles have happened, and I am happy. I no longer have problems but opportunities to love. I no longer have adversity but growth opportunities. This is not just a word game or a game of positive thinking or simply seeing the world through rose colored glasses. It is real problem solving through the power of love.

God's will is love

I have always wanted to know what God's will is for me, seeking his input on what school I should go to, what neighborhood we should live in, or what job I should take. I have wanted to know his will in all that I do, and for the most part, I believe that I have been led and directed. However, there have been those times when I must have heard wrong, because things didn't turn out the way I had expected. I began to think that maybe I had not been listening; maybe I was unworthy or I needed to repent for some wrong. Surely if I had received guidance and inspiration from God then things would have turned out better. I have since learned that this is not the case. God's guidance and inspiration is always for the greater good. Instead of experiencing only easy and smooth experiences, I may have needed to learn something greater—something of a higher worth. What I learned was how to surrender and depend on God instead of depending on my own strength.

Having cancer was a frightening and painful experience, and after seven cancer-free years, I found another tumor with a new type of cancer. Wasn't once enough? As I experienced both diagnosis and treatments, I had a very deep feeling that I needed to learn something—a feeling that I needed to *become* something through the experience of having cancer. It was frightening the first time, and even more frightening the second. I have learned so much by having cancer, and it has become two of the greatest experiences of my life. I needed it to become happy. Just like Adam and Eve, I needed to taste the bitter to know the sweet. I have met and talked to a lot of people who are waiting for God to speak to them before taking action so that they know his will. This waiting for God to speak, though a very good thing, causes many of my friends to experience anxiety and concern over their relationship with God. I used to think that I was so special that God had a very unique plan for me—a plan that would be revealed based on my worthiness and obedience. My mindset was that the plan for me was different from the people around me and that this made me special. I have since learned that God loves all his children the same. His love for them is great—beyond my imagination—but his love for each of his children is exactly the same. He is unable to bless me at the expense of someone else. His equanimity for his children demands that he consider the greater good and act accordingly. So here I am, going to work each day, doing the best I can, living a good life, and waiting for God's will to be revealed. My thinking was that as soon as I knew my purpose in life I could pursue it with determination and righteousness. However, as I learn more of God and how he loves all of his children, I am finding that he is more concerned about what is going on inside of me than what is happening on the outside. His will for me has more to do with the condition of my heart and mind than it has to do with the condition of my house, my car, or my job. God's will has already been revealed to me, and it is both simple and magnificent at the same time. God's will for me, God's will for you, is the same: his will is to love. Through love all things are accomplished. God is the creator. God is love, and therefore, all things were created by love. Love disarms the ego and returns you to your divine nature so that you can become whom God intended you to be instead of whom you have determined yourself to be. The more you embrace love as your only purpose in any situation and surrender the rest, the more the rest will embrace you. As it relates to problems and adversity, the secret sauce of the Happiness Factor is love. Love is like the water thrown on the Wicked Witch of the West in *The Wizard of Oz*. When drenched with water, the Wicked Witch dissolves. Love dissolves all negativity, discord, conflict, anger, contention, fear and strife. In all things, in all places, in all circumstances, love is all that matters. Love is all that is real. As I said earlier, when we do our part, God will do his. In every situation—in every circumstance—our part is to make love the most important factor in our lives. When we love—when we surrender to love—God will take our five loaves and two fishes and turn them into whatever they need to be. The worry, the contention, the fight, and the striving for possessions and control are all dissolved. When the ego is dissolved, just as water dissolves the Wicked Witch of the West, we are free of bondage to the ego. We realize our own potential, and we are able to be more effective. When we just love, we become part of the overall flow of the universe, great good happens to us and those around us, and we are happy.

Love versus fear

I have resisted the thought that all actions are either an expression of love or fear. Never considering myself a fearful person, I just could not accept the fact that I acted out of fear. That was before I learned that fear has many faces; the face of fear is found in selfishness, greed, envy, jealousy, anger, emotional pain, and even addictions. The face of fear is found in how I treat others and how they react to me. While I didn't consider myself fearful, I was certainly not free from being selfish or angry. I even had moments of jealousy, envy, and greed, confirming the existence of fear in my life. Consider that all of our emotions and actions can be placed on a continuum with love on one side and fear on the other. While our actions and emotions are rarely "pure love" or "pure fear," they are most likely somewhere in between. As I started to pay more attention to my emotions and reactions, I had to admit that I was operating more from a territory of fear than within the territory of love.

Whenever we stray from love, we enter into the territory of fear. Fear is best considered a state of lovelessness, or in other words, a crying out for love. Each encounter, each interaction, is either love or a cry for love. Love is magnetic and attracts all that is good. Fear repels, pushing people, success, and peace away from us. If I am greedy, I am fearful that I won't get what I want. When I am selfish, I am afraid of losing what I have. If I am angry, my fear can come from a myriad of sources, ranging from fear of abandonment to fear of a lack of trust to the fear of being hurt. It is all fear. Mother Theresa said, "The hunger for love is much more difficult to remove than the hunger for bread."[38] Just like we feel hunger for food, if we can recognize when we are afraid and see it more as being hungry for love, we can then shift to operate from the territory of love and allow God's healing process to take place. Many people I talk with think that acting in love is weak. But it takes more courage and more strength to love than to fear. Love has become so associated with sex and physical satisfaction that we have a hard time thinking of love as a powerful force in the universe. It is God's power—a power that can heal and dissolve all fear.

We need to stop thinking that life is based on some sort of rational equation where everything needs to balance out. We strive to "get even" and to make sure others "get what they deserve." Love cancels out the need to get even, and surrendering the situation to God leaves it up to him to judge as he sees fit. As I started to look at the emotions underneath my angry responses, I saw many faces of fear that I had not recognized before. Anger is an outward expression of lovelessness in the form of fear. You can justify being mad and angry all you want, but at the end of the day, you are crying out for love. You are afraid. The sooner you recognize this and address the fear, the sooner you can move back along the continuum to the territory of love. When we start to move toward love through compassion, kindness, and mercy, all of that and more comes back into our lives. We find there is really nothing to be afraid of. We are fearless as we love.

Love is all there is

We all want to be loved, and yet so few of us will admit it. It is an innate desire to be wanted and loved. If you want to be loved, you must start by loving, and loving begins with loving yourself. You cannot give what you yourself do not have. You may think you are extending love, you may feel you are loving others, but really you are only filling a void in yourself. That void will be filled with something. People fill that void with food and suffer with being overweight. Others fill that void with drugs, alcohol, and other destructive behaviors. Until you can feel natural and humble love for yourself and accept that you are who God intended you to be, you will not love fully. Once you love yourself, the love you feel will naturally extend to those whom you care most about. Love will then grow as you give it away and will eventually extend to your enemies.

I remember buying a 1978 Classic Volkswagen convertible, thinking it was unique because there were so few on the road. Once I bought it, I started seeing more and more of them on the road. I hadn't noticed them before I bought my own. Just like my car, when we open ourselves up to love, we start to notice it more readily around us. Love is magic, because the more we give away, the more we have. Several years ago I attended a church-sponsored father-son campout. As part of the evening program, our church leaders led the group away from the campfire to where it was dark. There was no moon that night, and we all felt the darkness gather around us. We were each given a candle and from the flame of a single candle the other candles were lit. We were asked to notice that one candle's light did not diminish as the other candles were lit, but the light in the circle grew as each candle was lit to join the others. This same thing happens as we give love to others. Our love is not diminished when we give it away; it joins the love of others. A life without love is like a candle that is not lit. God says not to hide your candle under a bushel; your light is love. Don't hide it or hold on to it thinking that you will not have it if you give it away. As you light your candle and let your love shine upon others, you will find that you have more light within yourself, which will cast out all your fear. You sill soon find you no longer feel as selfish, jealous, or greedy. You will learn to respond with love instead of anger. You will find lasting peace and be happy. It is lasting because it originates from the inside, not from the outside. As I said earlier, I have a fascination with stories of ordinary people doing extraordinary things. Love is the ultimate superpower empowering each of us to do extraordinary things. Love has the power to heal all hurt, all wounds, and all emotional pain. It has power to assuage all your fears. This power is already inside you, and you only need to recognize that it is there to release it and allow it to grow. The ego has disguised it as something you think is weak, telling you that you will be a sissy for loving. But the opposite is true. The greatest power to resolve differences, dissolve fear, dissolve problems, and combat adversity is love.

Fear is also a separation from God. The farther away we are from God, the closer we are to fear. Fear disconnects us from those around us. No one acts in isolation. No act of love is without positive consequences in your life and in the world. No act of fear is without negative and unpredictable consequences. As we learn to love, we realize that we are all connected. To harm or hurt someone else, we are mostly causing harm to ourselves. We are all connected by love as an unseen energy that touches all of us. Few of us, however, feel connected to ourselves, and so it is difficult to connect with others. We strive for intimacy with others but avoid intimacy with ourselves. The ego guards against knowing yourself too well; it avoids self-intimacy and creates fear of what you might find inside yourself. One way to become intimate and therefore connected with yourself is to live a life of integrity with a goal of not harming or hurting others physically or emotionally. Live a life of making and keeping promises, especially promises you make to yourself. The goal of living should be to live a life of love. Too often we compartmentalize and categorize life into several different "selves." We are one person at work, another person at church, another at home, and another with relatives and family. We create rules for each "self" that justifies our behavior. For instance, someone may feel justified in stealing from work but would never steal from a department store. Someone may lie at home but would not lie at work. Living with integrity connects all of these "selves" into one, and that connection opens up your heart and mind to love—a love that will extend to others. Once we connect with ourselves, we want everyone to live happily, and we will do our part to empower them.

Connecting with yourself through integrity uncovers a force of love that can dissolve fear, anger, guilt, abuse, and addiction. Connecting with yourself is not an act of conceit or pride; it is actually the foundation of love for all people. What is it we see in others? We see ourselves! If you don't like what you see in those around you, it is a reflection of how you feel about yourself. Learning to love yourself is a lesson in how to love others. Learning how to let go of personal judgment is a lesson in not judging others. Learning to have compassion and forgiveness for yourself is a lesson in forgiving others.

The power of love

Love is energy that is felt by all living things and creatures. As you develop love, you may notice that your pets respond to you with tenderness, babies will be calmer in your presence, and your plants or garden will be healthier. Those around you will notice it and feel more peace than they did before. In my early twenties, I worked with Benjamin Martinez. You could consider him my coach and mentor—he had a profound impact on my life. Ben Martinez was the type of person that you "felt" when he entered a room. The atmosphere in the room changed to be more positive, people were more optimistic, and there was less contention. By his nature, he had the ability to transform situations to be more peaceful. Having worked by his side, I knew firsthand that the source of this feeling was his ability to love. His love affected everyone he came in contact with. Perhaps you too know someone whose presence can be felt when you are near to them or when they enter a room. This sensation is the power and influence of love. It surrounds people who extend their love to others. Love follows those whose primary purpose in life is to love. When love becomes more important than anything else, others feel it, and they in turn will feel more loving and accepting as well. Some people report having a euphoric feeling when they first fall in love. They start to feel better about themselves, find better health, a better outlook on life, and have more energy. Some people even report greater spirituality. Sadly, the euphoria that comes with romantic love does not last without learning how to make it last. That same euphoria and sense of well-being can be experienced over and over again by developing love that is based in wanting the best for others, compassion, kindness, and a desire to not harm them. Love that originates on the inside and is not based on whom we are with, whom we see, or whom we desire is the kind of love that can create lasting happiness.

I am sure that at least one time in your life you have felt the love I am speaking of. Do you remember how it felt? If you visualize the circumstances, does that feeling of love return to you? How does it feel? I am sure you have felt the warmth of genuine caring—of someone's kindness and compassion. Think about a time when you felt this love, and dwell on it. Try to feel what you felt in that moment, and hang on to that feeling for as long as can. You may need to keep the thought in your mind. Commit that feeling to memory so that you recognize it when it comes back again. One way to commit this feeling to memory is to associate it with something physical. As you think of the time when you felt love touch your ear lobe or twist a ring on your finger, the feeling will be imprinted in your mind so that when you touch your ear or twist your ring, you will re-live that feeling any time you need to be reminded that you have felt the power of love in the past.

Imagine having an intense feeling of love any time you desire. Imagine feeling that way all day long. Sounds incredible, doesn't it? But it is not incredible; it is possible and quite probable as you practice and use the Happiness Factor. That feeling of love is energy that can be harnessed and directed toward others. When I first started meditating, I would recall a time when I felt intense love and allow myself to feel the warmth of that experience once again. I would then let that thought expand and allow that warm glow to spread throughout my entire body and consciousness. I was training myself to feel love and to create an emotional imprint of the feeling. During the day, I would then extend that love to someone I cared about. It was not a mental exercise so much as a physical exercise where I actually felt love flow from me to the other person, even if that person was not physically present.

I remember one night I was meditating to allow the love of God to flow into me. It filled me, and I felt peace and warmth all over. I directed that love toward my son Andrew, who was studying in the next room. In a rush, the door to my office burst open, and Andrew came in asking if I was okay. I was more than okay. I was feeling tremendous peace. I asked him why he came into my office, and he said he didn't know but felt that he needed to come in to see me. Further questions revealed that he was not anxious or fearful; he felt that he needed to see me but didn't have the right words to explain what he was feeling. For me, feeling love is very similar to feeling the Holy Spirit, feeling the love of God. It is like feeling the warm glow of a campfire and then mentally and physically extending that warmth, that love, to others.

In any situation, emitting loving thoughts and feelings toward others will have a definite impact. You will find less contention and greater peace. You will find that people respond to you with kindness and will go out of their way to take care of you. When I extend love through loving feelings and thoughts to my children, they react with greater respect. The same is true for people at the grocery store who become more pleasant and coworkers who get along better. Meetings at work are more effective, and better solutions can be found. You never love in isolation. When you feel love, it is felt by the person to whom you direct it and by those around you. Just like a pebble thrown into a pond creates a ripple effect, love ripples physical energy to others. The same can be true for you. Love is powerful and not only does it dissolve problems and adversity, it can also increase the kindness and love others feel in your presence. You will feel healthier, you will be more positive, you will find greater confidence and security, and you will be happy.

Love—sine qua non

Sine qua non is a Latin phrase, which literally translated means "without which, not." It is used to describe an indispensable action or condition. Love is the *sine qua non* of happiness. Love is the *sine qua non* of the Happiness Factor. Love is all there is. Though it sounds cliché, it is nevertheless true. Everything else is unreal; it is dispensable, fleeting, and situational. Regardless of the situation or the circumstance, regardless of what someone else has said or done to you, your response can and should be to love.

Love is the combination of emotional generosity and spiritual generosity and a return to your divine nature—a nature so divine that it cannot be destroyed. It existed before you were born and exists within you now. It can only be hidden, forgotten, disguised, and veiled by the ego. The life we live is the life we know. Start with loving thoughts; start by seeing beauty around you; start by forgiving others; start by surrendering all things to God and his power. Sometimes we take a strange comfort in misery. We get used to it, and although painful, it becomes our comfort zone. Breaking out of this comfort zone requires a new way of thinking. As you start to see the world differently and feel the desire to love, you may feel some discomfort. Persevere and you will be richly rewarded. You will need to stop being the victim. Loving, like happiness, is a choice we make. Making that choice is a great enabler for happiness.

Last year my son and I needed to return one of his Christmas gifts to the store. My wife was quite efficient that year and had bought the gift on sale in October. More than three months later, we were returning it because it was defective. The store was out of the model we had purchased and only had a more expensive model available. To make matters worse, the item was no longer on sale, and there was a long line of customers at the service desk. The person helping us was frustrated and irritated. Turning to my son I said, "I want you to pay attention to what happens here. I am going to pour as much love as I can into this situation and see if it makes a difference." As my son and I stood at the counter, we were helped by a woman who was frazzled and impatient. The last thing she needed was another problem. As I talked to her, I continued to extend feelings of love toward her and all around me. She was more helpful to us than she was to the others she had helped previously. With a quick phone call to the store manager, she was able to offer us the sale price from last October. Just as she was completing the transaction, she literally stopped what she was doing and said, "Wait a minute," as if something had just occurred to her. She took a small card out of her pocket and scanned it. She looked up at my son and me and smiled. I asked her what she had just done and with a big smile she said, "I just gave you an additional 10 percent discount. Just because I could." I looked at my son, hoping he caught what she just said. The look on his face showed he not only caught what she said but he really got it. He felt it too. My son and I now have a code phrase that means to extend love wherever you go: "Go for the extra 10 percent." The Happiness Factor is about going for that extra 10 percent. But this is not about a discount; this is about so much more. Love dissolves all negativity, and as it does, the negativity is replaced with love and other great benefits like the extra 10 percent. Would you like an additional 10 percent? What about 20 percent, 30 percent, or 50 percent more love in your life? What would you give for greater peace and happiness in your life? You only need to give one thing: love.

Love dissolves disharmony and conflict and allows peace to flow between people. Have you not been touched by love? Have you not been touched by the smile of another, their kindness, or friendly gesture? Have you not found beauty at one time or another? All of that is love, and if you have felt it once, you can feel it again. Better yet, you can help others feel it too. As you extend your own love toward other people, their behavior changes. It is softer and kinder. Love has that effect on the world. Love is *the sine qua non* of happiness, *the sine qua non* of the Happiness Factor.

Practicing love

It is easy to get caught up in the idea that love is a romantic feeling. Love is an action verb, and it has the power and force to mend relationships, heal emotional wounds, and remove all fear, worry, and even stress. Love enables you to be happy.

- Take a few minutes and start a list of the people you will encounter or interact with in the next few hours. Then go down that list and think of each person in the most positive frame of mind you can imagine. Let the positive feeling expand and fill your body, and direct it to the person's name on the list. Then, when you see or meet with that person, bring that feeling back and extend it into the encounter. You will be amazed at the outcome. Don't think that this is for personal relationships only. Any interaction between you and someone else will improve because of love.

- Do the above exercise with each person on the list, and then expand the list to the people you will see or meet tomorrow, the next day, and so forth.

- Perform the same exercise with people you feel closest to, then to people you feel neutral about, and then finally to the people you consider to be your enemies. As you do this, you will find you no longer have enemies. A life without enemies is a happy life.

Points to remember

- Love is energy. Energy that will dissolve all that is negative in your life.

- Every action is either love or a cry for love

- God's will for you is to make love the top priority in all you do.

- As you love yourself, you will love more fully.

The Happiness Factor

Chapter 10
Putting it all together

The Happiness Factor is living a life of love. It empowers you to be happy and empowers you to help others be happy also. It is the culmination of all that is written in this book. It is about making the choice to be happy, the choice to see things differently, to be forgetful and only see what is good and positive. It is the choice to forgive, the choice to live an abundant life and mindset, and the choice to surrender. It is also choosing to underreact, and it is the choice to love. Loving and being happy is not just sugar-coating. It is learning to skillfully relate, cope, and dissolve all that is negative in our lives. There are many people who live in favorable circumstances who are nonetheless miserable. Loving and being happy is about learning that peace is available in any situation, regardless of the circumstances. This peace comes through first learning and then practicing the concepts in this book. All of the concepts I have written about are embodied and enabled by love. When all is said and done, love is the Happiness Factor.

The Happiness Factor is a process, not an event. It is a set of lasting principles that do not change as the circumstances or situation changes. The Happiness Factor empowers you to stop living a life of dissatisfaction and unhappiness and to start living a life of happiness. You can rise above judging and criticizing others to living a life of forgiveness and peace.

You learn to love yourself and to love God and surrender all to him. I am happier than I ever dreamed, and my happiness is lasting and powerful. My circumstances have not changed tremendously. The outside is not that different, but the inside is very different. Miracles have happened that have brought me greater confidence, security, and abundance. The Happiness Factor is available to you—you can be happy no matter what. You cannot "find" happiness like a pot of gold at the end of the rainbow. Instead, you will *be* happy and experience greater satisfaction.

My hope is to put this together in a way that you can apply immediately and use often. As explained in the first chapter, using the P·E·A·S·E·F·U·L framework is an easy and effective way to recall the principles of the Happiness Factor. You can use it this way: whenever you feel your peace ebbing and flowing away, whenever you are in a situation that is best served by the Happiness Factor, you can simply say, "I choose to be P·E·A·S·E·F·U·L," and then apply the principles of the Happiness Factor.

The P·E·A·S·E·F·U·L framework is organized graphically by a circle that represents a continuous process rather than a step-by-step approach. You can start anywhere in the circle using one or all of the principles. Now that you have read and have started to enjoy being happy through the principles of the Happiness Factor, you can use any principle that suits the circumstance. Situations may call for love, and others may require you to change your mind or change your perception in order to be happy. Regardless of the circumstances, you can always apply the Happiness Factor to bring peace to your life. As explained in the first part of the book, the P·E·A·S·E·F·U·L framework is meant to be an easy-to-remember method of dissolving contention, negativity, and adversity. You could start your day with P·E·A·S·E·F·U·L as your guide in inviting God to be your partner. The P·E·A·S·E·F·U·L framework is meant to be unforgettable, easy, and actionable without a lot of words or memorizing.

The Happiness Factor

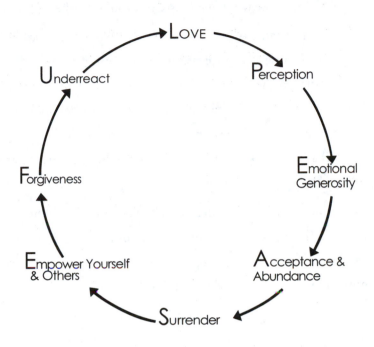

I will now give a summary of the P·E·A·S·E·F·U·L framework. You can refer back to this easy-reference guide whenever you need to.

P is for Perception

How we see our world is not how it is but a reflection of who we are. When we base our perception on the ego, it is easy to blame others and our circumstances for being unhappy. Perception is reality. It is your reality, and it is the reality of everyone around you. When we change our perception, we change our circumstances. When you sense a lack of peace or feel contention, changing how you are looking at your circumstances can bring you peace. Here are some suggestions to help you look at things differently:

- Think of someone who you believe to be causing you contention. As you think of this person you will change your perception by asking God to help you see this person differently. You could pray, "Help me see this person as God would see them."

- The grass is greener where you water it. Rather than avoiding a situation because it is unpleasant, try watering the grass before you venture to the other side of the fence. To change your perception you can admit that you are biased, and then look for an alternative. Strive to see the situation differently. You can say, "I know that I am biased, and I am willing to look at this situation differently."

- Our mind can be wounded much like our body when it is injured. The wound in our mind causes us pain. A simple prayer can help: "God, I am feeling pain, and my mind is wounded. I give you permission to heal my mind."

- An important aspect of perception is our frame of reference. Many people create a frame of reference based on their profession: "I am a banker" or "I am a morning person." You can change your perception by adopting your divine nature as your frame of reference. In a situation today say to yourself, "I am who God created, I am not the ego, I am not my profession, and I am a child of God." Today your happiness is up to you. It is not about anyone else; it is all about you. Make the choice to be happy.

E is for Emotional generosity

Emotional generosity is the quality of being *kind, welcoming,* and *understanding* of people around you in all of their limitations, imperfections, and flaws. Emotional generosity means that you give other human beings the benefit of the doubt, that you cut them some slack, and that you are slow to be harsh, condemning, or judgmental. Emotional generosity is the greatest act of generosity you can offer someone because it is an offer to give of your "self." Here is how you can practice being emotionally generous:

- In all of your interactions today, remind yourself that you are equal to everyone. We are all children of God, so you do not need to impress anyone.

- Today, make it a priority that you will not speak first in any conversation. You will be surprised at how much you learn and how much the other person appreciates it.

- Start your day tomorrow with this thought: "God, show me who I can be of service to."

- In the next few hours, express appreciation to at least one person. Call them on the phone if you have to. It will bring both of you peace

- Examine your thoughts, and consider how many negative thoughts you have. They are just that, negative thoughts. Then make them positive by being compassionate and kind in your thoughts about others

- Look at something innocuous and continue to look at it until you see the beauty in it.

A is for Accepting what is and Abundance

Accepting "what is" and abundance are two important principles of the Happiness Factor. Acceptance does not mean agreement; it is a way to get past denial and into action. So often, we try to understand things that we can't understand, and we end up keeping ourselves in denial. As long as you are in denial, you are unable to resolve the situation and let miracles happen. We also need to live in real time because we are where our thoughts are. Here are ways to accept what is and live in real time:

- When you are lost in thought, consider where your thoughts are taking you. Are you in the past? Are you anxious about the future? You are where you think you are—focus on the moment and be in the present.

- Consider one thing that you are concerned about. Now accept it for what it is. This is not agreement but acceptance. You might pray, "God, I accept what is and ask for your help to resolve this problem."

- Don't wait for quality time. Prioritize now time over quality time, and it will become the best time.

- Abundance is the mindset that there is plenty for everyone. It is an escape from greed, jealousy, and envy. Here is how to apply abundance in your life:

- The law of attraction is such that you attract into your life what you think about, so change your thoughts to an abundance mentality. Think of the positive things you want to attract, not the negative.

- There is no comparison. Any comparison you make is not healthy. Simply refuse to compare any longer.

- Have a gratitude attitude. Find one thing you are grateful for in this minute. Dwell on it, and feel the happiness that comes to you.

- Think of the one thing you desire most. Now, with that thought in mind, use the four steps to abundance:

  o Conceptualize it.
  o Visualize it.
  o Experience it.
  o Surrender it.

S is for Surrender

You win when you surrender. It is a paradox, but it is true. Your worry and anxiety is wasted energy, and there is a higher power that loves you and is willing to be your partner. By surrendering, your problems are no longer your problems; they are no longer a trial but an opportunity. Surrendering is giving up on results, no longer prescribing the outcome, and letting go of control and manipulation. When you surrender your fears, relationships, problems, and adversities to your God, you can live a worry-free life. Two things are essential in surrendering: 1) accept that there is a higher power, and 2) accept that without this higher power you are helpless and powerless.

- Take a few minutes to acknowledge your higher power, and in your mind, package up a problem and give it to God. He will accept it and then inspire you how to resolve it. You could pray, "God, I acknowledge your power, and I acknowledge that I am helpless to resolve this situation alone. I surrender it to you."

- Fishes and loaves: Our part is to surrender to God what we have, not to go out and acquire more. Surrender comes in a simple prayer, "God, I only have five loaves and two fishes. I surrender them to you. Please guide me to do whatever else you require. I surrender to you, knowing that you will make up the difference."

- The next time you are in an argument or you start to defend your position, simply surrender the need to be right. You can say, "I am willing to consider that I am not right, and I surrender the need to be right."

- You do not need to be afraid of anything. Surrender your fears to God. "God, I am afraid. My mind is wounded, and I surrender my fear to you."

E is for Empower yourself and others

Being happy requires your active participation. As you do your part, God will do his. The Happiness Factor empowers you to be more productive and effective by leaving the heavy lifting to God while you do what you can. Often we think that God will come to our rescue or help us only *after* we have done all we can. God is your partner *while* you do all you can. Our doing may require us to do things that are hard, uncomfortable, or outside of our comfort zone. However, you are now empowered to see and handle those things as opportunities rather than problems. Empowerment comes as you live a life of kindness, compassion, trust, and generosity. Just do what you need to do with God as your ultimate partner in accomplishing what you intend. It is the worry and the anxiety that we no longer need to experience as we do our part. We are empowered to go forward in faith, knowing that God will only do what is best for us. Our part is to be an active instrument in God's hands. You can empower others to be happy as well by living the Happiness Factor and sharing it with them. You will not be happy in isolation. Your own happiness has power to encourage and help those around you to be happy also.

- As you interact with others today, extend your own positive feelings of happiness into the situation. Your own happiness has a ripple effect on those around you.

- When faced with a decision on whether to help someone, determine if you are pleasing them just to make them happy or truly serving them. Then find the adequate level of service.

- Live by your moral code. Have integrity and be honest. Make and keep promises. When you listen to the voice of your divine nature over the voice of the ego, you are empowered to be happy.

F is for Forgiveness

Every offense has occurred in the past and only lives on in your memory. To a certain degree, when we hold a grudge, we are holding on to the past and letting it control our emotions and thinking. The ego needs to hold grudges as a survival tactic and as a way to try and convince us that we are more important than others. Self-importance is a myth; we are all equally important. Forgiveness will bring you unimaginable peace and confidence. Your mind will become clear, you will be able to love more deeply, and you will find peace. You will be healthier and have more energy. However, you cannot give what you don't have. Forgiveness is a choice to let go of the past and become more concerned about your own peace and happiness. Healing cannot occur in the past or the future. Healing happens now.

- Today, take a moment to consider something you do not have inner peace about. It is likely you need to forgive yourself for a past mistake, error in judgment, or a poor decision. Forgive yourself now! Don't wait. You could say this: "Had I known better, I would have made a different decision. I forgive myself and ask God to make up for the hurt I have caused others."

- Practice selective remembrance. You don't need to hang on to past memories that cause you pain, especially memories of the offenses of others. Let them go. Here is a way to get started: "I choose to have selective remembrance and to only remember positive aspects of the past. I ask for the miracle to forget any offenses, and I forgive and release those who have offended me."

- Choose to see only the positive traits of those around you. This can be accomplished by saying, "Today I will have partial blindness, and I will see the positive traits of others. I will be blind to their imperfections and inadequacies and will live without judgment."

- Today, ask for the miracle to see people as God sees them and to only consider their divine nature. "I ask for the miracle to see others as God sees them—to only consider their divine nature and to recognize that anything else is unreal."

- In a quiet place, start to forgive those you care about most, then those you have neutral feelings for, and then those who have offended you. As you do this, all those you need to forgive will come to your mind, even your enemies. As you forgive, you will find a burden lifted off your shoulders, enabling you to walk taller, feel lighter, and be happier. You will find you have no more enemies. You will be happy.

U is for Underreacting

Overreacting chases peace away. It is difficult to be happy when you are "freaking out" over something, even if it is important. Underreacting is a way to develop a more appropriate response in any situation and in any circumstance. "I choose to underreact" is an empowering statement that can bring peace to any situation. Underreacting is a skill that can be learned like any other skill. It is learned by practice, so start today. Choosing to underreact means choosing peace and love over anything else, and you will find great power in underreacting. Here are some tips to help you learn to underreact:

- Today, don't make any split-second decisions. Take the symbolic and magic three days of the resurrection. Just as the miracle occurred for Jesus of Nazareth, you will find miracles enter your life, and your problems will dissolve.

- Always expect the best in any situation. However, peace will come by accepting what is and then mildly neglecting. Nagging only brings contention and strife. Make it your motto to "Expect the best, accept the rest, and mildly neglect."

- Take a moment right now to identify your emotions. Are you feeling frustrated, angry, or depressed? Assess what is underneath those emotions, and recognize that happy thoughts can chase those emotions away and lift your mood.

- Your response to anything is in your control. You own that gap, and you can choose your reaction. Mind the gap!

L is for Love

Love is all that is real. Anything and everything else is an illusion. Any action or response is either love or a cry for love. We either operate from a fear-centric position or a love-centric position. Love brings with it the power to dissolve all negativity and conflict. God's will, in any situation, is to simply and purposefully love. When we stray from love, we feel jealousy, envy, strife, and contention. Love attracts kindness, security, peace, and affection and is activated by extending it to others in any situation. We often think of love as a feeling between two or more people, but it is more than that. Love is the energy and power to transform a situation. It is the ultimate superpower. Regardless of what someone has said about you or done to you, your response should be one of love. Love is the combination of emotional generosity and spiritual generosity. We all have love to extend to others. Make love an action, not just a feeling. Love is eternal and cannot be destroyed but sometimes lays hidden and dormant. Awaken your love by first loving yourself and then making love the only purpose in any situation. Soon, your problems, adversities, and negativity will dissolve, and you will be happy.

- In your very next encounter, make love your primary purpose. Regardless of the interaction, make love a priority and pay attention to the outcome.

- Tomorrow, make love your primary purpose in every situation.

- Accept that God's will for you is first and foremost to love. Love above all else. Don't let the ego tempt you or coax you into feelings of greed, jealousy, or envy. Just love.

- As you go about your day, recognize when you are acting from love or from a cry for love. You can be happy by seeing this in others as well. You begin to see them in their innocence instead of their guilt. Innocence brings peace, compassion, and love.

- Love is the *sine qua non* of happiness. Without it, there is nothing.

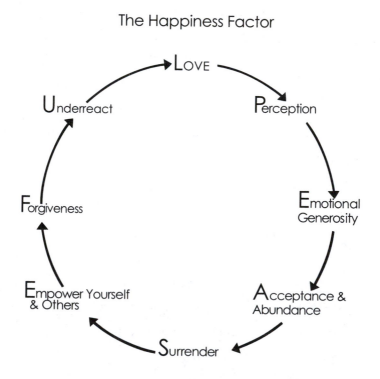

The Happiness Factor

Endnotes

[1] Lewis, *The Last Battle*, 210.

[2] Brickman and Campbell, "Hedonic relativism and planning the good society."

[3] Ireland, *Secrets of a Satisfying Life*, 31, 48.

[4] Covey, *The 7 Habits of Highly Effective People*, 69–70, 98, 103, 219.

[5] Williamson, *A Return to Love*, 271.

[6] Easwaran, *The Dhammapad*, 78.

[7] Williamson, *A Return to Love*, 104.

[8] Ireland, *Secrets of a Satisfying Life*, 31, 48.

[9] Dyer, *The Power of Intention*, 173.

[10] The Arbinger Institute, *Leadership and Self Deception*.

[11] Emoto, *The Hidden Messages in Water*.

[12] Hawkins, *Power vs. Force*, 101.

[13] Covey, *The 7 Habits of Highly Effective People*, 98.

[14] Covey, *The 7 Habits of Highly Effective People*, 103.

[15] As quoted in Hendrix, *Getting the Love You Want*, 279.

[16] Alexander, "Generosity."

[17] Liang, Krause, and Bennett, "Social Exchange and Well-Being," 511–523; Luks, "Doing Good: Helper's High," 34–42.

[18] Gautama Siddhartha, the founder of Buddhism, quoted in Medvescek, "Staying Healthy with a Chronic Disease."

[19] Tolle, *The Power of Now*, 82.

[20] Friedreich's Ataxia online parent support group, http://fortnet.org/fapg.

[21] Covey, *The 7 Habits of Highly Effective People*, 235.

[22] Gray, "The Common Denominator for Success."

[23] Covey, *The 7 Habits of Highly Effective People*, 219.

[24] Young, et al, "The Relationship between Objective Life Status and Subjective Life Satisfaction with Quality of Life," 149.

[25] Williamson, *A Return to Love*, 53.

[26] Oprah Winfrey, "Oprah on *The Color Purple*."

[27] Bassett, *From Panic to Power*, 147.

[28] Powdthavee, "Mental risk-sharing in marriage."

[29] Hawkins, *Power vs. Force*, 101.

[30] Ferriss, "Religion and Quality of Life," 199–215.

[31] Williamson, *A Return to Love*, 175.

[32] Clements, "Flipping a Coin."

[33] Worthington, "Research into the Strength of Forgiveness."

[34] Ramanaiah and Detwiler, "Life satisfaction and the five-factor model," 1208–10.

[35] Goleman, *Emotional Intelligence*.

[36] Covey, *The 7 Habits of Highly Effective People*, 309–310.

[37] Covey, *The 7 Habits of Highly Effective People*, 69–70.

[38] Desmond, "A Pencil In the Hand of God."

Bibliography

Alexander, Scott W. "Generosity." River Road Unitarian Universalist Congregation. http://www.rruc.org/sermons/sermon060319.htm.

Arbinger Institute, The. *Leadership and Self Deception: Getting Out of the Box*. San Francisco: Berrett-Koehler Publishers, Inc., 2002.

Bassett, Lucinda. *From Panic to Power: Proven Techniques to Calm Your Anxieties, Conquer Your Fears, and Put You in Control of Your Life*. New York: Collins, 1997.

Brickman, Philip and Donald Campbell. "Hedonic relativism and planning the good society." In *Social comparison processes: Theoretical and empirical perspectives*, edited by M.H. Appley. New York: Wiley/ Halsted, 1977.

Clements, Noah A. "Flipping a Coin: A Solution for the Inherent Unreliability of Eyewitness Identification Testimony" (March 10, 2006). *bepress Legal Series*. Working paper 1113. http://law.bepress.com/ expresso/eps/1113.

Covey, Stephen R. *The 7 Habits of Highly Effective People*. New York: Simon & Schuster, 1989.

Desmond, Edward W. "A Pencil In the Hand of God." Interview with Mother Theresa. *Time*, December 4, 1989. http://www.time.com/ time/reports/motherteresa/t891204.html.

Dyer, Wayne W. *The Power of Intention*. Carlsbad: Hay House, 2005.

Easwaran, Ecknath. *The Dhammapada*. Tomales: Nilgiri Press, 1993.

Emoto, Masuro. *The Hidden Messages in Water*. Hillsboro: Beyond Words Publishing, 2004.

Ferriss, Abbott L. "Religion and Quality of Life." *Journal of Happiness Studies* 3, no. 3 (2002).

Gray, Albert E.N. "The Common Denominator for Success." http://www.thinkarete.com/wisdom/works/essays/1462.

Goleman, Daniel. *Emotional Intelligence: 10th Anniversary Edition; Why It Can Matter More Than IQ*. New York: Bantam, 2005.

Hawkins , David R. *Power vs. Force: The hidden determinants of human behavior*. City: Hay House, 2002.

Hendrix, Harville, *Getting the Love You Want: A Guide for Couples*. New York: Harper & Row, 1990.

Ireland, David B. *Secrets of a Satisfying Life: Discover the Habits of Happy People*. Grand Rapids: Baker Books, 2006.

Lewis, C.S. *The Last Battle*. The Chronicles of Narnia. New York: Harper Collins, 1984.

Liang, J., N. M. Krause, and J. M. Bennett. "Social Exchange and Well-Being: Is Giving Better than Receiving?" *Psychology and Aging* 16, no. 3 (2001).

Luks, A. "Doing Good: Helper's High." *Psychology Today* 22, no. 10 (1988).

Medvescek, Christina. "Staying Healthy with a Chronic Disease." *Quest* 9, no. 3 (June 2002). http://www.mda.org/publications/quest/q93mindBody.html.

Powdthavee, Nattavudh. "Mental risk-sharing in marriage." Presented at the Royal Economic Society's Annual Conference, Nottingham, UK, March 22, 2005.

Ramanaiah, Nerella and Detwiler, Fred. "Life satisfaction and the Five-Factor model of personality." *Psychological Reports* 80 (June 1997).

Tolle, Eckhart. *The Power of Now: A Guide to Spiritual Enlightenment.* Novato: New World Library, 2004.

Williamson, Marianne. *A Return to Love.* New York: Harper Paperbacks, 1996.

Winfrey, Oprah. "Oprah on *The Color Purple*." Oprah After the Show. http://www.oprah.com/tows/after/200211/tows_after_20021122. jhtml.

Worthington, Everett L. "Research into the Strength of Forgiveness." A Campaign for Forgiveness Research. http://www.forgiving.org/ Campaign/harness.asp.

Young, D., et al. "The Relationship Between Objective Life Status and Subjective Life Satisfaction with Quality of Life." *Behavioral Medicine* 23 (1998).